THE
OKEFENOKEE
SWAMP

THE
OKEFENOKEE
SWAMP

A NATURAL AND CULTURAL HISTORY

MARIE LATHERS

THE
History
PRESS

Published by The History Press
Charleston, SC
www.historypress.com

Copyright © 2024 by Marie Lathers
All rights reserved

Turpentine dipper near Waycross, Georgia, 1937. *Dorothea Lange, Library of Congress Prints and Photographs Division, FSA/OWI Collection.*

First published 2024

Manufactured in the United States

ISBN 9781467157667

Library of Congress Control Number: 2024935291

To my grandmother, who took me to the Okefenokee.
Gladys Dorcas Turner McLendon
Jackson, Ohio, 1899–Waycross, Georgia, 1979

CONTENTS

ACKNOWLEDGEMENTS

I've been fortunate to meet many generous and knowledgeable people who have contributed much to the Okefenokee Swamp and surrounding area and also contributed much to this book. Whatever errors there may be in this book are mine; whatever appeal there may be in it is, in large part, theirs.

I owe a great debt to those who work at the Okefenokee National Wildlife Refuge. From my first unexpected meeting with Kimi Birrer to Larry Woodward's willingness to drive with me to local spots to take photographs, ONWR employees were patient, happy to help and wonderfully lively about all things Okefenokee. Sara Aicher, a refuge biologist from 1991 to 2022, met with me several times and meticulously went over part I of this book. Michael Lusk, the manager of the ONWR, and Larry Woodward, the deputy manager, provided materials, answered questions and shared their enthusiasm for this natural wonder. Kimberly Birrer, a biological science technician, also contributed. All three contributed striking photographs to this book.

At the Stephen C. Foster State Park, park manager Bryan Gray spent time explaining to me the differences and connections between the State Park and the National Wildlife Refuge. Alex Werner and Quinton Hutchison, interpretive rangers, guided me on boat tours, one to Billys Island. I'm grateful to them all.

At Okefenokee Swamp Park and Adventures, cultural interpreter Leslie Ranew was especially informative and supportive. Levi Welling, the director of operations, and Katie Antczack, a RESA education coordinator and science education coordinator, gave important input. I also enjoyed meeting Kim Bednarek, the site's executive director. Matt Rouse and Jenny Smith, boat guides, also helped me understand the swamp.

I benefited by doing research at the Waycross Okefenokee Regional Library (Ware County), which maintains an impressive collection of books and other materials about the Okefenokee Swamp. Several days in the Special Collections at the Zach S. Henderson Library of Georgia Southern University were invaluable, and I thank Autumn Johnson and Willow Farmer for their assistance with the papers and photographs of Francis Harper in the Delma E. Presley Collection. Kathy Lafferty of the University of Kansas Kenneth Spencer Research Library, Alex Boucher at the University of Alabama Special Collections and Archives and Deborah Davis at the Valdosta State University Archives and Special Collections helped me procure images. The online resources of the Charlton County Historical Society were also helpful. Many individuals have generously given permission for me to use their photographic and other images in this book; their names appear in the illustration credits.

I was unable to meet with Chris Trowell before he died, but his extraordinary output about the history and culture of the Okefenokee Swamp constitutes a veritable treasure trove for any scholar or layperson who is seriously interested in the swamp.

My meetings with descendants of Swamper families were valuable and meaningful. I visited with Edwin Griffis at Griffis Fish Camp, still open for business near Fargo, and we had a delightful conversation. Sheila and Charlene Carter, descendants of Chessers, Carters and Roddenberrys (Charlene is the owner of Okefenokee Pastimes), visited Chesser Island with me and shared family stories. Several years ago, I also had the pleasure of visiting with Luther Thrift and his wife in their home. At that time, Bobby Tatum was kind enough to take me on a boat trip to Billys Island. I also met then with Sue Clark, grande dame of Waycross, who authored a book on the Okefenokee Heritage Center. More recently, I had the chance to visit with Charles Eames, the former head librarian at the Okefenokee Regional Library in Waycross.

A chance meeting with Sandra Dixon at the High Bluff Primitive Baptist Church in Brantley County, Georgia, was most memorable. She invited me to Saturday and Sunday services and explained the workings of the church. She also made sure I went home with a hymnal. A visit to the Mars Hill Primitive Baptist Church in Hoboken, Georgia, deepened my understanding of Sacred Harp music.

Marward Howard and her son Josh Howard of Friends of Okefenokee National Wildlife Refuge, a group that provides significant service to the ONWR, were very welcoming. Member Jim Holler took me on an informative tour of the inside of the Chesser homestead. I'm pleased to share 25 percent of my profits from this book with that organization for its continued efforts.

I owe a big Okefenokee thank-you to Walt and Ginny Frazier of Woodbine, Georgia, for their friendship over the years and for Walt's wonderful photographs of the swamp.

Finally, I am grateful to Joe Gartrell, my editor at Arcadia Press/The History Press, who has been more than supportive from the moment I inquired if the press would be interested in such a book.

A word about the text: Readers will note that Billys Island is sometimes spelled Billy's Island in citations and titles from other authors. Indeed, there is no common spelling of this island; I have chosen the one most used by government agencies. Billy's Lake, however, retains the apostrophe. Floyds Island is almost always spelled without an apostrophe, as it is in this book.

INTRODUCTION

Although the Okefenokee National Wildlife Refuge regularly welcomes large numbers of visitors from around the world, there are people who express confusion when the Okefenokee Swamp is mentioned to them: "The what? Okey-dokey Swamp? Do you mean the Dismal Swamp? Wait, is that where Pogo lives? I didn't know that was a *real* swamp!"

I love introducing people to the land of the trembling earth and its unusual habitat and inhabitants. The Okefenokee's water—how perfectly reflective it is, its color, its acidity, where it comes from, where it goes—is a distinctive feature worth highlighting. The American alligator, one of the swamp's most significant residents, is known to all, but there are few places where specimens can be seen with such frequency. Orchid fanatics appreciate knowing that fringed orchids, rare in most areas of the United States, can be spotted in the Okefenokee's moist sphagnum moss. The largely untold story of the Black members of the Civilian Conservation Corps company that constructed the foundations of the Okefenokee National Wildlife Refuge arouses much interest. *Star Trek* fans appreciate knowing that Gene Roddenberry was a member of an old swamper family; although he never lived near the Okefenokee, many Roddenberrys still do. Even avid movie buffs may not be familiar with both film versions of *Swamp Water*, the novel by South Georgia author Vereen Bell, much less the 1971 feature film *Swamp Girl*, set in the Okefenokee. And finally, how many people living on the East Coast are aware that the cypress wood in their older homes and furnishings may well have been culled from the Okefenokee? If this book serves a purpose, it will open more eyes to these and other uniquely fascinating features of the Okefenokee Swamp.

But where to begin? The 438,000 acres that form this large basin constitute a big apple to take a bite out of. In a gesture toward digesting our current understanding of the swamp, this book is divided into three parts, each focusing on one of its realms: natural, historical and cultural. As a counterweight to generalizations and summations, the book is punctuated by more detailed comments on particular species and stories, like the Okefenokee Zale moth, the infamous "knees" of pond cypresses, the Queen of the Okefenokee or Walt Kelley's comic strip *Pogo* about an opossum who lives in the swamp. Hopefully, readers will walk away with a broad sense of what this wetland is and what it means to those who live near it, with at least a few of its characteristics remaining in their memories. Hopefully, they will then ask their neighbors and friends, "Have you ever heard of the Okefenokee Swamp?" and be able to recite some amazing facts and stories.

The Okefenokee Swamp, located in southeast Georgia and northeast Florida, is a freshwater and blackwater wetland and the largest ecosystem of its kind in North America. Called a "swamp," the Okefenokee is really a wetland with both bog and swamp features. It is a thirty-five-by-twenty-five-mile depression that is about two feet lower than the surrounding uplands, making it distinct from river swamps, which may also be blackwater swamps but form along the banks of large rivers. The average depth of the water in the Okefenokee is two feet, and it is the source of two rivers, the Suwannee and St. Marys. The most impressive feature of the Okefenokee is its hydrology—the way its waters flow—which, unlike the waters of the Everglades, the Great Dismal Swamp and other wetlands of North America, has remained, for all intents and purposes, as it was thousands of years ago. Such a distinction calls for concerted efforts to maintain the water system for future generations, and such an effort is currently underway to prevent mining around the rim of the swamp.

The Okefenokee National Wildlife Refuge (ONWR) is the largest National Wildlife Refuge east of the Mississippi River. It encompasses almost all (93 percent) of the swamp, for a total of 406,000 acres. Although what remains of the Great Dismal Swamp in Virginia and North Carolina is larger than the Okefenokee, its National Wildlife Refuge is almost 300,000 acres smaller. For comparison purposes, the ONWR is half the size of the state of Rhode Island. Most of the swamp is also designated as

National Wilderness Area. National Wildlife Refuges fall under the U.S. Fish and Wildlife Service, a bureau distinct from the National Park Service, although both are under the Department of the Interior. A significant distinction between a National Wildlife Refuge and a National Park is that although visitors are welcome at refuges, they are less of a priority than they are at parks. National Parks are areas conserved, in large part, for human recreation, whereas wildlife refuges work to protect wildlife habitats. This does not mean, however, that visitors will not feel welcomed at the ONWR.

In addition to the National Wildlife Refuge entrance on the east side of the swamp, visitors may access the Okefenokee at the Stephen C. Foster State Park on the west side. The National Wildlife Refuge leases 134,000 of its acres to this Georgia park. A third main entrance is the Okefenokee Swamp Park (OSP), a nonprofit, located on the north side, near Waycross. Currently, the ONWR and the OSP are involved in a partnership to advance a bid to UNESCO to name the Okefenokee Swamp a World Heritage Site. Entities that have already recognized the special status of the Okefenokee include the National Audubon Society and the International Dark Sky Association. The 1990 Clean Air Act acknowledged the pure air of the swamp. In addition, the swamp's 120 miles of navigable waterways form part of the National Water Trails System. It's no wonder that just ten years ago, *National Geographic* recognized the Okefenokee as number 49 of the 100 "World's Most Beautiful Places" on our planet.

Home to over 850 plant species, 233 species of birds, 101 species of reptiles and amphibians, 39 species of fish and 49 mammal species, the Okefenokee Swamp hosts only one invasive species, the wild hog, the result of farming and ranching conducted on some of its largest islands and in the surrounding area. These living creatures, along with the sedimentary features and chemical reactions that characterize the wetland, contribute to the swamp's special scents, sounds and dazzling array of colors. These aspects change according to the seasons, as the swamp traverses spring, summer, fall and winter. A visit to the Okefenokee in one season is a sensual experience all its own, and returning in a different season leads to surprisingly new impressions. Like all vital wetlands, the Okefenokee and its surrounding uplands are in a state of constant change, yet along with new revelations remain bounties that can be relied on—the sound of a red-cockaded woodpecker carving its cavity in a longleaf pine, the grunt of an alligator bull during mating season, the sunshine color of the yellow pond lily flower and the earthy smell of peat.

Those fortunate enough to experience the Okefenokee will tell you that it is a place like no other, a refuge for the species that depend on its soil, water and air to thrive. We are invited in but only for short spells. This world belongs, after all, to the Okefenokee fishing spider, the prothonotary warbler, the little brown skink, the pond cypress, the Spanish moss and the fetterbush vine.

PART I

NATURE

1

QUIVERING EARTH

We can thank Benjamin Hawkins for leaving us a succinct paragraph about the meaning of the word *Okefenokee* to the Natives who lived in southern Georgia at the turn of the nineteenth century. In 1796, Hawkins, a statesman from North Carolina and a delegate to the Continental Congress, assumed the role of principal Indian agent to the Muscogee people, who were called Creeks by the English. For his era, Hawkins was enlightened in his dealings with the Muscogee, enmeshing himself in their culture and mastering their language. In his reports, he summarized the various names of the swamp in use in the last years of the eighteenth century:

> *The O-ke-fin-o-cau is the source of the St. Mary's and Little St. Johns, called by the Indians Sau-wau-na. It is sometimes called E-cun-fin-o-cau, from E-cun-nau, earth; and Fin-o-cau, quivering. The first* [name] *is the most common amongst the Creeks. It is from Ooka a Chactau word for water, and Fin-o-cau, quivering. This is a very extensive swamp, and much of it a bog; and so much so, that a little motion will make the mud and water quiver to a great distance. Hence the name is given.*[1]

For Hawkins, the quivering land was a swamp dominated by a bog, one whose soggy terrain responded promptly to any slight movement of its waters.

The early Spanish, French and English settlers who traveled through southern Georgia and northern Florida attached versions of this Muscogee name to their own terms for wetlands—*laguna* (Spanish); *marais* or *marécage*

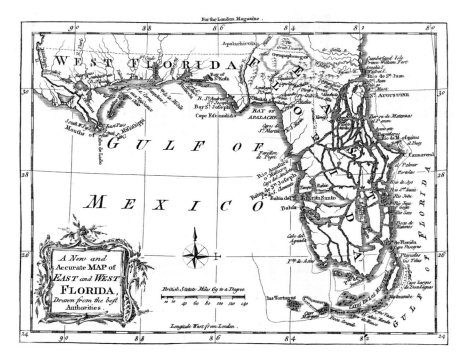

"A New and Accurate Map of East and West Florida, drawn from the best authorities." "The Great Swamp called Owaquaphenogaw" appears over the location of the swamp. London Magazine, *1765; courtesy of the University of Alabama Libraries Special Collections.*

(French); and *lake, morass* or *marsh* (English)—to refer to the Okefenokee region. Sixteenth- and seventeenth-century maps show the use of their terms, including Laguna de Oconi, Le Grand Marais d'Owaquaphenogaw and the Great Morass. Over time, *swamp* won the contest from the range of other English words used to describe wetlands, among them *bog, fen, peatland* and *marsh.* Although not all the Okefenokee is technically a swamp—as will be discussed further on—the term stuck. And over time, *quiver* has given way to *tremble.* Still, today, the Okefenokee Swamp is known as the "land of the trembling earth."

The transliteration of a Native term for *quivering land* into the Roman alphabet and then into English has an entangled history of its own, one that continued to preoccupy people into the twentieth century. In the early 1920s, an ecologist at Cornell University, Albert Hazen Wright, transcribed some eighty distinct spellings of the name of the swamp that had been used since 1763. These included Owaquaphenogaw (1763), Akenfonogo (1795),

Hawkins's Okefinocau and Ecunfinocau (1799) and Eokenfonooka (1810). Wright wrote that although it was not possible to settle without reservation on one specific form, he recognized Hawkins's terms as the most definitive and chose Okefinoke—with an "i" and single "e" at the end—as his preferred rendition of Okefinocau, relying on the pronunciation of the settlers living in the Okefenokee rim. Tied for second place, Wright listed Okefanokee and Okefenokee.[2] Francis Harper, a Cornell biologist who kept detailed records of his visits to the swamp from the 1910s to the 1930s, preferred the spelling Okefinokee, as reflected in *Okefinokee Album*, the name given to a collection of his writings and photographs.[3]

In the late nineteenth and early twentieth centuries, the quivering Swamp of the Southeast was far from the only U.S. location whose name and spelling were debated. To settle matters, the federal government created the Board on Geographic Names to standardize place names in the century-old nation. This board's volume of place names, decided between 1890 and 1932, records the following: "*Okefenokee*: swamp, Florida and Georgia. (Not Akenfonogo, E-cunfino-cau, Ekanfinaka, Okeefonokee, Okefenoke, Okefinoke, nor Oquafanoka)."[4] As suggested by this quote, it was necessary to list the terms that needed to be phased out to ensure that maps and histories be drawn and written with the regularity demanded by a modern, scientific country. This acquaintance with the various names of the swamp used over the decades—indeed, over centuries—is a fitting starting point for our present journey into the natural, historical and cultural realms of the Okefenokee.

The Okefenokee is its own space, a truly distinct terrain that can resist precise scientific and common-sense classifications. It offers a unique, even eccentric, natural environment that is unmatched in quality and distinctiveness by any other wetland east of the Mississippi. Moreover, beyond ecological classifications, the Okefenokee adheres to our cultural assumptions concerning swamps. It is home to cypress trees, their knees jutting up from the water and Spanish moss cascading from their branches; pond lilies flaunting white or yellow flowers; alligators that sunbathe in the daytime; and the melodies of pig frogs and barred owls who serenade all of the swamp's species in the evening. The Okefenokee readily fulfills our contrasting mental images of swamplands as, on one hand, foreboding, primeval spaces characterized by dangerous, even monstrous, encounters between humans and nature and, on the other hand, peaceful, Edenic and even welcoming spaces that preserve nature in its most innocent form. A more balanced view sees the Okefenokee as a wetland that is not fully one or the

An Imaginary View of Okefenokee in 1832. Woodcut by R. Brookes published in the New Universal Gazette, *1848, 562; Z. Smith Reynolds Library Special Collections and Archives, Wake Forest University.*

other but rather a dynamic terrain where life forms synchronize themselves like an orchestra in a perpetual cycle of growth, decay and regrowth.

In the recent draft "Statement of Universal Value" for the proposal to make the Okefenokee National Wildlife Refuge a World Heritage Site, the authors wrote, "The heart of the property is the Okefenokee Swamp, the largest headwater precipitation–fed swamp within the subtropics and the most complete example of a large, un-fragmented, naturally driven freshwater wetland on the North American Coastal Plain."[5] Compared to the two other large freshwater wetlands east of the Mississippi—the Great Dismal Swamp in Virginia and North Carolina and the Everglades in Florida— the Okefenokee boasts the most pristine ecological conditions. Although humans have encroached on it over the last 150 years, the swamp remains governed by natural water fluctuations and periodic droughts and fires. The Okefenokee is a dynamic habitat undergoing constant change, change that now occurs, fortunately, with only very slight human interference.

Concerted efforts were made in the late nineteenth and early twentieth centuries to transform the natural state of the swamp, but they were ineffective; the Okefenokee is, in terms of land mass and major features, what it was thousands of years ago. By definition, wetlands are transitional areas between solid land and large bodies of water; they may have salt water, fresh water or a mixture of both (brackish water). They are usually divided into four categories: marshes, swamps, bogs and fens. Bogs, also called peatlands, and fens are permanently saturated, and their water comes from precipitation (bogs) or underground springs (fens). Marshes are consistently flooded by surface water and groundwater but cannot support trees. What distinguishes a swamp from a bog is the depth and stagnation of the water. Also, in a freshwater swamp, one can find woody plants, including trees. Certain parts of the Okefenokee do support forest growth, with pond cypress, oak, tupelo, bay, black gum and pine trees growing there, as well as woody shrubs. These are true swamp areas.

Swamp waters are mostly stagnant, however, and this is not true of Okefenokee waters. While the swamp may appear immobile to the casual observer, its waters do flow. Galileo purportedly said under his breath that while the Earth seems immobile to humans, "it moves," and we might say this of the Okefenokee. Due to differences in land elevation, more of the Okefenokee water moves westward than eastward, making the Suwanee River more substantial than the St. Marys River. Canoers and kayakers notice this current while out on the water trails of the Okefenokee. This "swamp" is not stagnant. In addition, the Okefenokee, unlike a true swamp, is a headwater of the two rivers previously mentioned. This movement and outflow into the rivers, along with the approximately fifty-two inches of rain that annually fall on the Okefenokee (accounting for 70 percent of the water entering the swamp) is a primary reason for the purity of Okefenokee's water as compared to typical swamp water. (Although most of the rainwater is lost to evaporation and evapotranspiration from plants and soil, rain remains the major source of the swamp's water. The remaining 30 percent comes from runoff from the surrounding land.)

The Suwanee River crosses state lines and eventually empties into the Gulf of Mexico, while the St. Marys River sends its waters to the Atlantic Ocean. The fact that most of the water flows west confused explorers and would-be developers of the area, who found this to be counterintuitive. When, in the late nineteenth century, for example, Henry Jackson attempted to drain the swamp into the St. Marys River, his workers were bewildered to see that the water was determined to flow west toward the Suwannee River. In addition, due to the cycles of drought and rainfall in the area, the water not only moves, but its levels are changeable as well. Whereas true swamps have low water levels without regular periods of

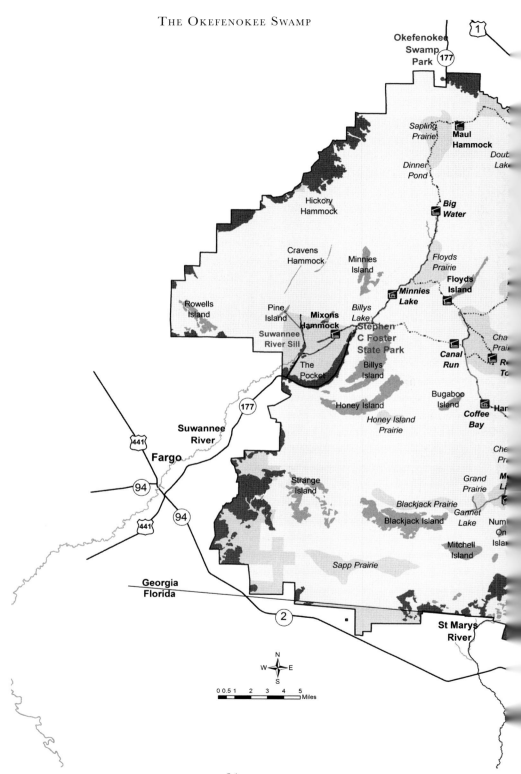

exposed soil, parts of the Okefenokee may dry up enough to impede even small boats from passing.

The Okefenokee area's formation as part of the Georgia Coastal Plain (a part of the North American Coastal Plain) began during the Pliocene era—six million years ago—with the deposit of sand and culminated in the Pleistocene era (two million years ago). At one point about two hundred thousand years ago, the Atlantic Ocean covered the present swamp's 400,000-odd acres (about 682 square miles). As the ocean receded following a period of cooling, large dune formations remained—what we now call barrier islands. In the Pleistocene era, these barrier islands were located farther inland than the barrier islands of today and included a long and wide ridge known as Trail Ridge. Trail Ridge defines the eastern edge of the Okefenokee. It runs 157 miles from Jesup, Georgia, to Starke, Florida, rises between 150 and 250 feet above the surface and is up to 2 miles wide in some places. Since the land on the ridge's west side is lower than the uplands around it, a basin or depression formed as the ocean receded and the remaining saltwater drained off. The basin began as a dry savannah with periodic fires; later, its bottommost parts began to collect rainwater, and this water then spread out. The uplands—pine barren savannahs—defined the rims of the bathtub, making it a perfect trap for rain.[6]

We might think of the Okefenokee as a renegade wetland protected by the stubborn Trail Ridge, which keeps it from flowing into the Atlantic. The St. Marys River flows from the southeast corner of

Okefenokee National Wildlife Refuge map. *UFSWS.*

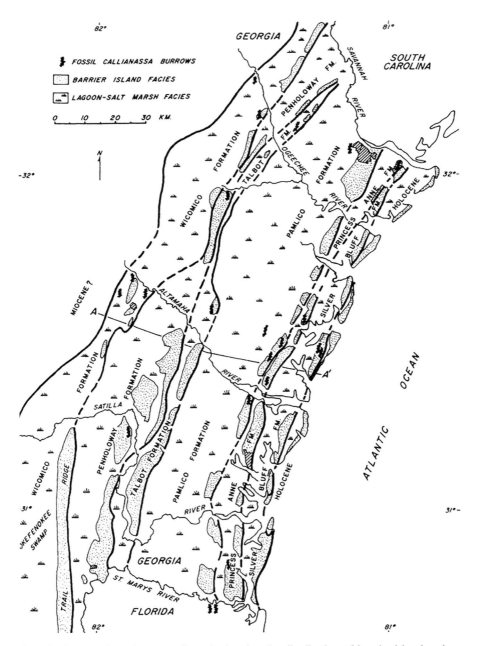

A geologic map of southeastern Georgia showing the distribution of barrier island and lagoonal marsh sediments in Pleistocene formations and Holocene sediments. *Figure 1 in John H. Hoyt and John R. Hails, "Pleistocene Shoreline Sediments"; printed with permission from Creative Commons.*

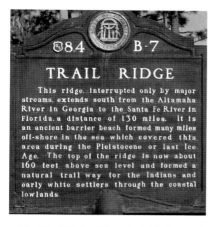

084 B-7

TRAIL RIDGE

This ridge, interrupted only by major streams, extends south from the Altamaha River in Georgia to the Santa Fe River in Florida, a distance of 130 miles. It is an ancient barrier beach formed many miles off-shore in the sea which covered this area during the Pleistocene or last Ice Age. The top of the ridge is now about 160 feet above sea level and formed a natural trail way for the Indians and early white settlers through the coastal lowlands.

The Trail Ridge Historical Marker off Georgia Highway 23. *Larry Woodward, USFWS.*

the swamp and passes through a low area in Trail Ridge before turning north and east toward the ocean. The Satilla and Alabama Rivers also cut through the ridge, near Waycross, Georgia. Trail Ridge creates, contains and "manages" the swamp by managing the water flow out of it and holding rainwater in. Without it, such a wetland would probably not exist in this area—at least not one as commanding as the Okefenokee. This explains why conservationists have made concerted efforts to prevent projects that might in any way trespass on Trail Ridge.

Visitors to the Okefenokee, especially the younger ones, want to know if the land really trembles. This is a good question, and the answer is a qualified "yes." The waters and trembling earth of the swamp are always in movement and ever shifting, although large enough islands remain stable. Animals and plants that thrive in the Okefenokee have adapted to this movement in ingenious ways, an example being the buttresses at the base of cypress trunks, which fan out to ensure balance. More precisely, though, the quivering of land masses is the result of a specific swamp process that creates new land from the bottom up. There are many islands in the swamp—large ones, such as Billys and Floyds Islands, and smaller ones like Chesser Island, which is still substantial. Animals such as the black bear, red fox and marsh rice rat depend on this stable land for foraging and nesting. Woody plants and trees also depend on and contribute to this stability. Humans, too, from those of the late Woodland period (900–1600 CE) to the Swampers of the nineteenth and twentieth centuries, have found enough firmness within the swamp to sow and reap crops, hunt and fish, drive cattle and build shelters. Smaller land masses that are younger and still in the process of forming are the ones that tremble, and this is because of something called peat.

Some islands of the Okefenokee have long formed part of the swamp and may be remnants of barrier islands, whereas some were formed more recently and owe their existence to peat. The peat that accumulates on the floor of the swamp is responsible for the creation of new land in the Okefenokee. We might say that it is the equivalent of the magma that rises from rifts in the ocean floor—from beneath the water, processes play out that push new earth to the surface. Peat does not form under Earth's crust; rather, it forms on the surface from decaying plants. There are several names for the land bodies found in the swamp. Peat batteries, also called floating islands, appear when peat dislodges from the swamp floor and rises to the surface, where it floats, and mixes with mud and aquatic plants. Loose, floating parts, or beds, of peat that only partially rise to the surface may also lead to the formation of batteries. Over time, a battery may become a "house," or a larger mass of quivering land that can begin to support shrubs and trees.

But what, exactly, is peat, and why does it form layers over the sand underneath it? When vegetation dies in the swamp, it falls most often in water, where it decomposes. Due to the anaerobic (lacking in oxygen) conditions of the water, this decomposition happens very slowly. In bogs and blackwater swamps, peat forms from this partially rotted vegetation. The primary plants that form peat are cypress needles, water lilies and, to a lesser extent, ferns and sedges. Most of the Okefenokee peat is some four to six feet thick, peaking at around twelve feet thick in some areas, and some of the layers are 6,500 years old. You might ask what stops this process from turning the entire swamp into relatively solid land. For one thing, drought may expose peat and reduce moisture within the vegetation, causing the formation of land to stop; fire also contributes to the containment of the peat. Thus, peatlands and swamp water remain balanced in the Okefenokee. Since decomposition in Okefenokee water is a slow process, however, it takes an average of fifty years for one inch of peat to form. Even centenarians live only long enough to witness two inches of peat form in the Okefenokee.

As noted, decomposing cypress needles are a major component of peat. Most cypresses in the Okefenokee are pond cypress, although bald cypresses can also be found. Cypresses are deciduous conifers, which means they lose their needles annually. Since cypress roots grow out horizontally instead of straight down, they, and the buttresses of the trees, contribute to moor the trees on ground that is unstable. Roots from various cypress trees in an area contribute to keeping the whole lot stable enough for them to gain quite a bit of height. It helps in this regard that cypress wood is lightweight. An area with many of these trees together constitutes a "cypress dome habitat." Cypress trees are adapted to the nutrient-deficient soil, and a layer of bark beneath the top layer of bark shields them from fire damage. As for the photogenic "knees" of the cypress tree, scientists do not yet understand their evolutionary purpose.

Cypress trees are perfect residents of the Okefenokee, and they give and take from their environment for evolutionary purposes. Due to past logging,

Cypress buttresses help stabilize these trees on the shaky ground of the swamp. *Michael Lusk, USFWS.*

Cypress buttress. *Larry Woodward, USFWS.*

however, the trees of the cypress forest in the swamp compose only about 10 percent of the Okefenokee today, and all but a few of these trees are younger than one hundred years old. Scattered old-growth trees were spared from logging because they were diseased, hollowed out or isolated from other trees. A few can be seen along canoe trails.

As with all conifer needles, pond and bald cypress needles add acidity to the water they drop into. This acidity comes as a result of the tannins in the needles. This returns us to peat, which forms from the slow decomposition of vegetation promoted by acidic water. The slow process is also caused by low levels of nutrients, including nitrogen and phosphorus, in the water. Low oxygen levels in the water, which also contribute to acidity, are caused by the slow movement of the water, which prevents the replenishment of oxygen. As a result, the swamp water's acidity (3.9–4.4 PH) is roughly equivalent to the acidity of orange juice. Bacteria are unable to flourish in this environment, making the water less dangerous to drink than it would be otherwise.

The slow decomposition of plant matter also leads to fermentation and the production of methane gas in the peat. This gas is virtually odorless since it disperses so quickly. This methane can create a sort of luminescence on the surface of the water that is referred to as foxfire. As methane fills the pockets or voids in the peat that sits at the bottom of the swamp, the pressure of its bubbles may build up. A layer of this peat may then rise or bubble up to the surface. Snapping turtles and alligators may also dislodge peat so that it will bubble up to form peat blow-ups, or floating islands, as has already been mentioned. Partially decomposed plant roots may still be attached to the bottom of the blow-up.

The naturally occurring compost island of peat is very attractive to aquatic plants that are looking to spread. Maidencane, a grass, is one of the first to arrive on a blow-up, stabilizing it with its roots so that it can eventually support bushes. The roots of water lilies, which can be up to five and six feet deep, may then become tangled or enmeshed in the peat, forming a thick weave of tubers and roots. To return to the question of the trembling earth, a battery may or may not be able to support the weight of a human; if it cannot support yours, you will notice a tremble just before you become soaked in swamp water. There is no "quicksand" in the swamp aside from these floating islands.

The water's absorption of light and the reflection of light off the smooth, mirror-like surface makes the water appear black. Dipping a transparent cup into it reveals, however, that it has a tan or light-brown color. This is

An aerial view of "houses," or areas of land formation, in the swamp. *Larry Woodward, USFWS.*

not due to pollution but to the tea-like steeping of dead plant material in it, as discussed previously. Still, there may be pollution in the water. Although the acidity of the water prevents many types of bacteria from growing in it, pathogens may still be present. And although the Okefenokee suffers from scant pollution, rain that is contaminated may carry pollutants into its waters. The Okefenokee is a headwater swamp fed mostly by rain, but streams to the northwest of it are secondary sources of water and may contain some pollution. This is all to say that it is best not to drink Okefenokee water.

2

SINGULAR CREATURES AND COMMUNITARIANISM

The Okefenokee is about 23 percent open prairies, 54 percent shrubbery and 18 percent forested terrain. These habitats are home to 850 plants, 426 vertebrate animals and an undetermined number of invertebrates. From the Florida black bear to the American alligator, the southern dusky salamander to the dusky pygmy rattlesnake and eastern pipistrelle bat, animals thrive in the swamp. Its onetime inhabitant, the ivory-billed woodpecker, is now, unfortunately, extinct; in addition, the Florida panther and gray wolf, both endangered in the United States, are gone from the swamp due to habitat changes and hunting. One can still find the eastern indigo snake, a threatened species, in the Okefenokee, despite the hunting of and loss of habitat for gopher turtles, the tunnels of which the snakes use for protection. The wood stork, although threatened, does appear in the swamp now and then.

As for plants, carnivorous pitcher plants, golden clubs and loblolly bay, swamp bay and sweet bay trees flourish in the swamp. Visitors can also find the white fringeless orchid, a threatened species. In addition, macroinvertebrates, such as midges, water mites and ondata (or "toothed") dragonflies, are at home here. Indeed, as in any ecosystem, Okefenokee plants and animals depend on each other for survival and propagation and depend on and contribute to the natural processes surrounding them, the filtering and flowing of the air and water and the cycles of drought, fire and rain.

The American alligator has no competition as the emblem species of the swamp. Only two species of alligator exist in the world, and ONWR remains one of the American alligator's most reliable habitats. (The other species is the Chinese alligator.) Due to overhunting for hides and sport, the alligator population diminished in the early to mid-twentieth century, and in 1967 the reptile was federally recognized as endangered. Happily, as with a few other plant and animal species of the swamp, the rejuvenation of this species followed the founding of the National Wildlife Refuge in 1937. By 2010, the alligator population was back to its pre-decimation state, and there are currently about twelve thousand alligators in the swamp. The reptile is now listed by the U.S. Fish and Wildlife Service as being "of least concern."

Visitors usually spy at least one alligator in the swamp, especially on sunny days between March and May, when the alligators are active. Despite common exaggerations, alligators generally have no interest in attacking humans—most of us are too large to make a meal of. If an alligator feels threatened, however, especially near a female's nest, it may attack. Certain alligators have had to be relocated due to becoming aggressive around boat docks and canoe platforms, but this is usually due to visitors feeding them at these sites. (Feeding animals in ONWR is prohibited.) You should always maintain a respectable distance from this animal, in part because alligators can, due to their tails, attain speeds of up to twenty miles per hour in water and even faster on land.

At birth, alligators have yellow stripes; as adults they turn black or deep olive, depending on the amount of time they spend in water. Interestingly, alligators have evolved an extra eyelid that functions like a pair of goggles. This allows them to see clearly in swamp water. Being outside of the water comes naturally to them, however, since they are cold-blooded and must spend time warming up in the sun. At night, their metabolism slows in the cooler air and they devote themselves to indulging in food. Subsequently, they begin digesting their meals once morning comes and their body temperature increases. Another fact about them is that although alligators are usually seen alone, adults (generally ranging from four to seven feet long) may form "congregations" near the water, while younger gators may hang out in "pods."

Mating season for alligators runs from April to early June. This is when visitors hear the rumbling grunts or bellows of males in search of females. The lower the bellow, the older the male. Mating females seek bulls larger than themselves, and the male's call reveals his size; it also informs other bull alligators of who their competition is. Originating in the lungs, the groan

A mother alligator with her young on her back sunning. *Larry Woodward, USFWS.*

elicits a vibration that causes water to "dance" over the animal's back. Most often heard at sunrise and sunset, the sound may travel more than a mile and may sound quite alarming to humans.

Around the end of June, females begin to lay their eggs at the edge of the water and then build nests of rotting vegetation around and over them. These clutches contain anywhere from thirty to sixty eggs, and each egg is three to three and a half inches long. A distinctive feature of the alligator is that the temperature of a nest determines the sex of the offspring; if a nest is over ninety degrees Fahrenheit, males will emerge; if it is between eighty-six and ninety degrees Fahrenheit, females will emerge; and if the nest is below eighty-six degrees Fahrenheit, both will emerge. This must be considered as naturalists gauge how climate change will affect this species. Babies hatch in August or September, and mothers stay with their young for up to a year. Growing a foot per year, those alligators that make it to six or seven years old are usually home free, as they are too large for a predator to eat them; 90 percent of hatchlings do not reach this stage, however. Alligators that reach this age may live into their thirties or even seventies, with a rare few growing older.

Alligators dig holes into the ground for the purpose of collecting water, especially during droughts. These water holes attract other species, thus providing alligators with a source of food. Still other species benefit from the holes for shelter and access to water. Overall, the alligator is a fascinating swamp creature that, instead of evoking fear in humans, should evoke endless curiosity and a good amount of respect. The size of the Okefenokee and its healthy habitat offers this reptile the opportunity to live as it was meant to live. It also offers us the chance to benefit from understanding the American alligator's intricate adaptation to its ecosystem.

Another large and usually nonaggressive animal of importance in the swamp is the Florida black bear. There are an estimated four hundred black bears in the Okefenokee-Osceola ecosystem. (The Osceola Wildlife Management area sits across the Florida border from the Okefenokee, with which it forms a wildlife corridor.) The ecosystem provides protection, food, adequate acreage and suitable spaces for reproduction. Swampers called these mammals "hog bears" because of their attacks on livestock. Due in part to these attacks, Swampers hunted bears in the latter nineteenth and early twentieth centuries, which, along with loss of habitat, led to their status as threatened; now, however, the species is labeled "recovered."

The bear's diet is varied and includes acorns, seeds and berries, as well as insects and small animals, including small alligators, although the bears eat more alligator eggs than hatchlings. They particularly enjoy eating fruit from the black gum tree, which grows throughout the swamp. In fact, the black bear's feeding habits also contribute to the maintenance of the black gum tree population, as bears deposit seeds throughout the swamp after eating the fruit. In a good year for these berries, bears stay in the Okefenokee in the fall and then hibernate or den in cypress trees through the winter. They may also hibernate in ground nests they build at the edges of the swamp. If the black gum berry crop is insufficient, however, bears will seek acorns from oak trees in the piney woods of the uplands, thus exposing themselves to hunters. ONWR, though, protects both black gum trees and bears within its boundaries, allowing the population of this important mammal to grow.

The black bear also appreciates a satisfying meal of alligator eggs, which leads to a codependent relationship between these two species. Although the bear is, in general, a threat to the alligator, as it will ingest an alligator's eggs, it also guards alligator nests from other predators, such as raccoons. Black bears also have a sweet tooth for turtle, or "cooter," eggs, as do other animals of the swamp. While the eggshells of the most common cooters are famously hard to break, a large bear will find success—if any is left over, smaller animals benefit. Turtle eggs are easier to find than alligator eggs, and alligators themselves are not averse to feasting on them. Sometimes, turtles will lay their eggs in alligator nests, and the female alligator will end up unknowingly protecting them. Thus, connections that benefit survival are significant between alligators, turtles and bears.

Unfortunately, the population of gopher tortoises was low at periods in the past due to settlers culling their eggs for food. Now, with protection, this is not an issue, although habitat loss continues. Known as a keystone animal due to its tunnels, which provide shelter for dozens of other species, these tortoises are necessary players in the Okefenokee community.

Intriguing animals of the Okefenokee that may not be familiar to visitors include the anhinga, the bowfin, the pig frog and the Okefenokee fishing spider. The anhinga is a large black waterbird that can be seen perching in cypress and other tall trees along with many other songbirds, waterbirds and birds of prey (of the latter, especially the red-shouldered hawk and barred owl). Often called "snakebird" by locals, the anhinga has a long, serpentine neck and a straight, pointy beak. The anhinga may be confused with the double-crested cormorant, whose beak is, however, slightly curved down at its tip. Its sharp beak makes the snakebird excellent at spear fishing. Anhingas often sit still on a branch with their wings spread wide to dry their feathers and raise their body temperatures; they must do this after spending up to six minutes under the cool water, stalking prey.

Bowfin fish, called "trout" by Swampers, are often too large and too fast for the anhinga. Quite common in the swamp, bowfins make a considerable noise when thrashing and jumping in the water in a movement called boiling. In fact, the sound of alligators dancing and bowfins boiling might be confused by the uninitiated. Like animals with lungs, bowfins must come up for air on occasion, and the gulps they take produce the sound. Like the Florida gar, also found in the swamp, the very primitive bowfin takes air in through its gills and a gas bladder; it can therefore stay out of the water longer than other fish.

The diversity of fish, reptiles and amphibians in the swamp is a sign of its water quality. Frogs are the loudest amphibians, drowning out just about every other noise in the Okefenokee in the afternoons and evenings of spring and summer. The frogs themselves do not seem to mind the overwhelming cacophony of brass instruments insistently resounding about them. Males respect their neighbors less than females, it seems, since most calls heard are from males as they strut their stuff for potential mates. Evolution has wired

The anhinga spreads its wings to dry them after taking a dip in search of food. *Larry Woodward, USFWS.*

females to hear their own species' call more strongly than others, making mate selection an easier process.

After the cricket frog, the most numerous of the approximately twenty species of frogs (including several tree frogs) in the Okefenokee is the pig frog. A nocturnal species, the aptly named pig frog grunts, making it a musical cousin of the grunting alligator. This frog calls out in verses composed of one to three vocalizations. It may be seen and heard as it peeks up over a pond lily pad in a lake or prairie. In fact, a lily pad may be underneath the pig frog, whose weight will push it down. There are American bullfrogs in the Okefenokee, but there are not many due to the water's acidity; so, what you may take for a bullfrog is almost certainly a pig frog. Pig frogs have a green, green-gray or green-brown color with white bellies and yellow throats (the latter in the male) and black or brown spots on their backs. They are not choosy eaters, which gives them prominence as swamp creatures who keep other species in check. Their diet includes plenty of species, among them spiders.

Orb-weaver spiders are sighted in the swamp during certain times of the year. These are the large spiders that visitors can literally run into as they walk on boardwalks, meander down trails or canoe along waterways. The female banana spider, also known as the golden silk orb-weaver, can spin an orb of spider silk (a web) that is up to six feet wide—or even farther if one counts the web offshoots attached to tree trunks. Most impressively, their silk is five times stronger than steel, tougher than Kevlar and more flexible than nylon. Another spider, one named for the swamp, is the Okefenokee fishing spider, which, unlike the orb-weaver, does not spin a web. Instead, this aggressive brown arachnid lives on tree roots and trunks. Instead of passively waiting for prey to become enmeshed in a web, these water striders actively stalk prey on the surface of the water or just under it. Among the largest spiders in the United States, the (female) Okefenokee fishing spider can have legs up to five inches long.

A distinct Okefenokee aquatic plant that is easy to identify is bladderwort. Resting on and just under the surface of the water, bladderwort has small pink or (more often) yellow flowers. The pattern of its filaments in the water resembles that of a human nerve cell or the root system of a large tree, although in terms of size, of course, the bladderwort falls somewhere between these two extremes. The plant is carnivorous, feeding on single-celled or multi-celled organisms by snaring them in tiny air-filled bladders, or sacs. Bladderwort also thrive on the bacteria and germs left when rainfall dilutes the acidity of the surface water; they essentially purify the water by ingesting these germs. Another common aquatic plant is golden club, a type of arum nicknamed "never-wet." The tiny hairs of this plant make it water repellent, rivaling the best raingear. Never-wets are easy to spot among the pond lilies and bladderwort in the spring, when their bright yellow flowers, which dot a spiked tip, shoot up above stalks that are green at the bottom and white at the top.

Maidencane is a grass that grows in the mid-Atlantic and southern states along lakes, ponds and swamps, and it is associated with the Florida Everglades. It is also a common sight in the Okefenokee. Reaching two to three feet in height, maidencane is rooted to shallow land but may extend

Sundew, a carnivorous aquatic plant. *Michael Lusk, USFWS.*

Yellow water lily, or spatterdock. *Larry Woodward, USFWS.*

a long way out into the water, especially when dead areas break off and float onto a lake. Mistaking it for land, however, can lead to wet shoes and pants. Maidencane grows along the main (constructed) canal that boat tours follow. When workers dug the canal, they tossed soil to the sides of it, leaving perfect spots for this grass to flourish. Alligators are often sighted partially exposed as they rest among maidencane, which provides them with a good amount of privacy.

Carnivorous plants thrive in areas with low-nutrient soil, like the Okefenokee. Eighteen carnivorous plants live in the swamp, including three types of pitcher plants, four sundews, three butterworts and eight bladderworts. The Okefenokee pitcher plant is a giant variety of the hooded pitcher plant and thrives particularly well in this swamp. It may reach a height of over three feet. Like the golden trumpet pitcher plant, it displays bright yellow flowers in the spring. It has a beautiful green "hood," often with red intermingled and bright red "lipstick" lining its opening. Trumpet pitcher plants are also especially tall. Insects become enmeshed in their open hoods, which do not lean over like those of the hooded variety.

There are, in addition, thirteen species of orchids in the Okefenokee, including rose pogonia and grass pink orchids. Both have small pink flowers. It takes some luck to see them, as their flowers do not last long. They emerge among the maidencane and other plants along water trails and on lakes. As already noted, the threatened white fringeless orchid is present in the swamp. A regional recovery plan is underway to maintain this orchid in the Southeast.

Interactions between the species living in the Okefenokee are often beneficial, sometimes for one of the species involved and other times for both. As they are everywhere, the flora and fauna in the swamp exist not as isolated lifeforms but as a community. The following are a few highlighted examples, as it would take a very long time to consider all the species that interact in the swamp. Readers should keep in mind that the entire ecosystem taken together is characterized by communitarianism, or the interdependence of living things.

A first example is the bromeliad, or air plant, with the misnomer Spanish moss, certainly the most iconic plant of the Okefenokee. Native to North America, the "moss" fascinates northerners, who are not used to trees that display fake beards made for elderly giants that have been washed and hung out to dry. There is a lichen in the swamp called old man's beard, but Spanish moss is neither a lichen nor a moss—nor was it imported from Spain. And despite what many believe, Spanish moss is not a parasite and does not damage the tree whose branches it hangs from—unless it really overwhelms it. Instead, it is an epiphyte, or a plant that grows on another plant. As a perk, it filters the air of pollen and humidity, thus benefitting the ecosystem.

Spanish moss does take advantage of a tree, certainly, to position itself optimally for absorbing nutrients from the air and rainwater. It also provides, however, protection and cover for small species of insects, spiders and birds. Certain birds may build their nests in it or use bits of it to build nests elsewhere. Tiny greenish-yellow flowers characterize the plant, and its seeds, once released, may attach to the bark of trees, creating the occasional hairy tree trunk. The idea that you should not touch Spanish moss because it harbors chiggers is true only if the moss has been on the ground. In fact, the only downside of Spanish moss is that its flammability may carry fire into treetops.

Several stories are associated with the origin of the name "Spanish moss." Some sources state that the original Native term for the plant is *Itla-Okla*, Choctaw for "tree hair." This is untrue, however. In Choctaw, *okla* means "people," but there is no word *itla*, although *iti* does mean "tree." The term in Choctaw for Spanish moss is *iti shumo*.[7] As for the origin of the English phrase, it can be traced to French colonists, who arrived in the sixteenth century. At some point, the French labeled the plant *barbe espagnole* (Spanish beard), surely in reference to the Spanish who had preceded them in Florida by a few decades. Some say the French colonizers shaved their beards, whereas the Spanish did not. Interestingly, the French word *mousse* means "foam" or "froth," while *mousse végétale* translates to "moss." Also, the word *moss* in Scottish may signify "bog," likely in reference to the sphagnum moss that is very prevalent in the bogs of Scotland, England and Ireland. This brings us full circle back to swamps—after a detour by way of facial hair!

The tree most associated with the swamp after the cypress is the pine. Slash pine grows on wet soils and is found in the swamp, while longleaf pines thrive in dryer sites, like islands and the uplands surrounding the swamp. When loggers harvested longleaf pine from the uplands, they often replaced it with slash pine, which they preferred because it grows faster. Unfortunately, only 3 to 4 percent of the original range of longleaf pine remains. This harvesting of pines has had a very consequential impact on an Okefenokee bird species, the red-cockaded woodpecker, the only woodpecker in the Southeast that builds its cavities in living pine trees. The federal government has listed this bird as endangered since the 1970s. In the Okefenokee area, this bird builds its dens in older longleaf and slash pine trees on islands and in the uplands. Specifically, it requires mature (fifty- to eighty-year-old) trees because of the softness of their wood caused by red heart disease; the woodpecker thus turns to its advantage what is detrimental to the tree. Other species of birds that are not able to make dens themselves but need them for reproduction also use these cavities. When logging companies harvest pine instead of allowing the trees to mature, this woodpecker loses out.

Red-cockaded woodpeckers live in breeding pairs with their previous year's offspring, although each bird of the pair requires its own cavity and, therefore, its own tree. Interestingly, the male red-cockaded woodpecker stays with the young for multiple years, while the female often leaves in the fall of the hatch year. Currently, the Fish and Wildlife Service is committed to growing longleaf pines on the perimeter of the swamp to promote the growth of the red-cockaded woodpecker's population. In addition, prescribed (or controlled) fires keep the habitat clear of too much understory for the woodpecker and other animals. Artificial cavities are also provided for woodpeckers, although not inside the National Wilderness Area. Finally, monitoring the red-cockaded woodpecker population outside the National Wilderness Area involves attaching colored bands to the birds' legs.

Another example of ecological communitarianism is the relationship between the fetterbush vine, cypress tree and Okefenokee zale moth. First, it is important to distinguish fetterbush from climbing fetterbush, which is the vine. Called the "hurrah-bush" by Swampers, fetterbush is an evergreen shrub in the heath family. It intermingles with thorny greenbrier vines in the Okefenokee to create dense thickets. Although they are in the same family as the climbing vine, the bush and vine are distinct species. Fetterbush is more prolific and the most noticeable, producing whitish-pink and pink flowers. As for climbing fetterbush, it also has delicate spring flowers. It grows along the lower parts of cypress trunks in particular, its rhizomes taking advantage of small openings in the tree's bark to dig in (without causing harm to the cypress). It is noteworthy that the leaves and nectar of both the hurrah-bush and the climbing fetterbush are highly toxic if ingested.

A moth of the genus Zale that thrives in cypress swamps, especially the Okefenokee, bears the name Okefenokee zale moth. ONWR is one of its favorite habitats. The larva, or caterpillar, is very colorful, displaying orange, black, and white stripes. The moth itself carries shades of brown, white and black and has a wingspan of about two and a quarter inches. The caterpillar's only food is the fetterbush vine, making it essential to the survival of this species. In turn, the caterpillar keeps the fetterbush vine in check so that it will not smother the tree trunk. Since the moth reproduces

Fetterbush shrub flower. The fetterbush vine has, instead, a cream-colored flower. *GLG/Stockimo/Alamy stock photograph.*

annually, the caterpillar population is not large enough to put the vine at risk of disappearing. Thus, the vine is dependent on the tree, and the caterpillar is dependent on the vine. These are essential relationships.

It is truly remarkable that the species of animals and plants presented here are a mere fraction of those that inhabit the Okefenokee. The substantial

Baby egrets in their nest. The Okefenokee is also home to green herons, pelicans, ibises and other water birds. *Larry Woodward, USFWS.*

number of species, combined with the size of the swamp, make it an incomparable natural ecosystem. Even though humans in the past worked hard to manipulate the area, the Okefenokee's resiliency contributes to its survival as an ecosystem that shelters, feeds and provides a stage for some of the most dazzling natural processes that define our world. It is not surprising that many scientists, conservationists and naturalists have devoted decades of their lives to this special place. The logging of the swamp has had long-term (in our lifetimes, not in geological terms) effects, but this is surface damage that can be repaired. It is imperative that we allow the swamp's recovery to continue by preventing any new nefarious human encroachment in the Okefenokee.

3

SWAMP FIRE

It seems counterintuitive that a wetland such as a swamp would suffer from regular fires, but this is the case in the Okefenokee. The prolific growth of vegetation in such a fertile environment combined with sometimes severe drought periods creates favorable fire conditions. In their 1926 *History of the Okefenokee Swamp*, A.S. McQueen and Hamp Mizell refer to a mammoth fire in 1840–41, one long remembered by old-timers who lived in the Okefenokee rim:

> The old pioneers still speak of the time when the Okefenokee Swamp "burned up" as they term it. It happened about 85 years ago and an old resident died a few years ago at the age of 96 who remembered well the occasion. He stated that, while he was a mere lad, he remembers it vividly, for the pioneers would talk of nothing else. He stated that the smoke hung over the entire country for several weeks, sometimes becoming so thick as to obscure the sun….It is [now] nothing unusual to haul out from bottoms of lakes and other places far in the interior of the Swamp, burned and blackened logs and stumps.[8]

This was the first recorded in a long line of Okefenokee blazes. Almost one hundred years later, the naturalist Francis Harper wrote a firsthand account of a fire that occurred in 1931–32:

> Appalling forest fires all about the last few days, even in the heart of the Okefinokee….Tom Chesser, who had gone out in the edge of the prairie

west of the north end of the [Chesser] *island, said he had to race for his life and was really scared; blazing hanging moss was blown ahead of him and set fire there....Both Ben and Harry Chesser declared emphatically that they had never seen "such a sight in their lives"—the swamp as it now is....Numbers of houses and barns were burned and destroyed between the swamp and Trader's Hill* [a nearby village] *a couple of days ago, as a strong west wind blew the blaze swiftly across the land.*[9]

Just a year later, though, Harper recorded that the swamp was making a comeback: "On our way to the island yesterday, it was an amazing and refreshing experience to find how green the country looks after last year's drought and fire. Even a mile or two out on the 'hill' [Trader's Hill], where everything on and near the ground was consumed or fire-blackened, there is a good green growth of grass and other ground plants."[10]

In addition to the 1931–32 blaze, notable twentieth-century Okefenokee fires were those that occurred in 1908, 1954–55 and 1990. The 1954–55 fire was the result of five fires merging and it burned over 318,000 acres in the swamp and 140,000 acres of uplands. This fire, one of the most significant

A controlled burn. Prescribed fires are meant to cleanse the understory but save healthy trees. *Michael Lusk, USFWS.*

in the recorded history of the swamp, occurred naturally. As often happens when fires break out, several blazes joined together, and much of the swamp was engulfed. After the devastation, Congress passed a "Swamp Bill" (in July 1956) that called for the construction of a 186-mile-long perimeter road around the swamp and a sill, or dam, at the headwaters of the Suwannee River on the west side of the Okefenokee. The latter was meant to maintain a stable water level in the Okefenokee to minimize the spread of fire. This idea had been around since at least the mid-1930s, when it was proposed as a way to increase the area's value as a waterfowl refuge. The sill was constructed in 1960.

By preventing erosion from the Suwannee River from entering the swamp and controlling the amount of water that flows into it, the five-mile-long sill did raise the water level. However, during droughts, when fires occurred, it backed up water in only 1 percent of the swamp. This was due to the natural terracing basins within the Okefenokee, which prevent the water from spreading out evenly. The water channel within the swamp that becomes the Suwannee River is a riverine system characterized by minimal peat buildup. But when the sill held water in the pocket area, plant material no longer floated downstream; instead, it fell into the water to form peat. Thus, peat formation occurred where it normally would not have, which may have increased the acidity of the water in this area. The large-mouth bass population seemed to suffer from this acidity. In addition, the sill never accomplished what it was intended to—decrease the number and extent of large-scale wildfires. To restore the natural flow and connectivity between the swamp and the Suwannee River, the sill's two spillways were opened in 2000, and in 2010 the earthen dam to either side of it was breached in three locations. One result of this breach is that large-mouth bass have since made a comeback.

So far, the Okefenokee area has known more than one megafire (over 100,000 acres burned) in the twenty-first century. The Georgia Bay Complex Fire of 2007, one of the largest fires in United States history, involved the merging of several fires over a period of three months. A downed power line just southwest of Waycross caused the initial blaze, the Sweat Farm Fire. One of the other fires that merged into the complex inferno was the Bugaboo Fire, so named because it started—due to lightning—at Bugaboo Island. In the end, 560,000 acres burned both inside and outside the Okefenokee National Wildlife Refuge in both Georgia and Florida. Six thousand area residents had to evacuate, and hazardous smoke conditions extended hundreds of miles, from mid-

Florida to the city of Atlanta. High winds and drought exacerbated the blaze, which continued until Tropical Storm Barry dropped enough water to extinguish it. Following this devastation, the Swamp Edge Break, a firebreak built around the perimeter of the swamp, was widened to allow for better access to and escape from such incidents in the future. It cannot, however, prevent fire inside the swamp from reaching the uplands. Additional helicopter dip sites or ponds were also constructed to facilitate access to water when needed; there are currently seventy-four such sites in the swamp area.

The Honey Prairie Fire of 2011 lasted three months and resulted in the burning of 90 percent (309,200 acres) of ONWR. The fire was not officially declared extinguished until April 2012. This fire was allowed to burn, and efforts to keep it within the boundaries of the National Wildlife Refuge, whose structures were successfully protected, were successful. One of the goals of fire management is to do just this—allow blazes that start naturally in the swamp to burn within it but not let them reach the uplands and surrounding inhabited areas. Finally, a blaze that will long be remembered was the West Mims Fire of 2017, which started by lightning and consumed about 152,000 acres. Changes in the natural habitat along the National Wildlife Refuge boundary due to human presence exacerbated this fire. In addition, high winds hampered suppression tactics, and the fire crossed the swamp's Edge Break. Of the total acreage burned, 32,000 were privately owned.

A reminder of the danger of firefighting was the tragic loss of Richard S. Bolt, a biological technician for ONWR, in 1979. To protect people at the Stephen C. Foster State Park, Bolt used a bulldozer to extinguish a fire in the Pocket area when fire reached him. Unfortunately, he died two weeks later, after suffering major burns. The visitor's center at ONWR is, fittingly, named for him.

The presence of fire can, of course, be harmful to flora and fauna. During an Okefenokee fire, certain animal species flee to unaffected land, while others hunker down for the duration. Either way, populations of some species of animals may suffer. Like plants, however, the animals soon return, appearing from their holes and returning from the uplands. The entire cycle of drought, fire and rain is extremely delicate but has evolved to keep an equilibrium among Okefenokee wildlife.

In the uplands, another way that the health of the Okefenokee depends on regular burnings is the release of conifer seeds from cones that require the elevated temperatures created by fire to do so. Fire also prepares the ground for the germination of plants in a general way: it clears the ground of fallen branches and other plant debris. Longleaf pine seeds, for example, do very well in this cleared soil. (The needles dropped by these trees can, however, help spread fire.) A final example of the ecosystem's dependence on fire comes from the woodpecker, in particular the ivory-billed woodpecker. Last seen in the swamp in the 1940s and now regrettably extinct, this bird depended on fire because the insects it ingested appeared only two years after a fire. Without regular burns, these woodpeckers would have lost a major food source. As for the red-cockaded woodpecker, which is making a comeback in the uplands due to management efforts, fires that are not very intense are crucial in providing them with open and low understory habitat. Overall, cycles of fire and drought are necessary to maintain the Okefenokee as a wetland. Without fire, the area would, over time, quickly become a woodland.

The three-stage cycle of wet periods, drought and fire results in fires occurring in the Okefenokee every seven to ten years, with larger ones occurring every twenty to thirty years. Nature does an excellent job of balancing fire and water in the Okefenokee through a cycle of naturally occurring—and now, managed—fires, which spread in drought periods, alternating with the quenching of fire by swamp water and rainy periods. Human intervention in this balance, unless carefully managed, can cause unfortunate harm to the ecosystem. One of the most significant effects of fire is that it "selectively" removes certain plants and trees, allowing others to grow unimpeded by competition for space and sunlight. Once a fire cuts back deciduous trees, shrubs and palmetto, their canopy will no longer impede the growth of grasses and forbs. This clearing of hardwood trees and shrubs from the Okefenokee generally skips cypress trees, however, which are fire tolerant. Thus, the majestic tree that we normally associate with swamps continues to characterize the landscape.

Saw palmetto, a common plant in the areas surrounding the swamp, is also adapted to frequent fires. While its leaves are very flammable, its rhizomes are mostly not affected, allowing it to sprout up quite quickly after a burn. Black bears, racoons, sandhill cranes and gopher tortoises are a few animals that eat the berries of saw palmettos, and the plant provides protection and coverage for several bird species and small mammals, amphibians, reptiles and insects. Fire plays a major role in all of this.

It is commonly thought that because Okefenokee peat is so thick and so susceptible to fire, when exposed by drought, peat fires may burn for a very long time, even over periods of many months. Although the peat is thick, most swamp blazes are surface fires that move rapidly across the landscape.

The fire tower at the Okefenokee Wildlife Refuge. *Michael Lusk, USFWS.*

Intense fires do burn into the peat in small areas—usually across less than twenty acres—where the peat has dried deeper down, as illustrated by some recently burned areas. The peat can smolder for months, but fire will not spread quickly until the heat returns to the surface and ignites vegetation. Even during a very hot fire, the root systems of peat are usually spared, since fires do not burn very far into them. When a fire depletes a large area, the resulting lowering of the peat bottoms can lead to the formation of new prairies, such as Chesser and Grand Prairies, or even lakes. In fact, the establishment of new prairies usually takes several fires and the right water depth conditions.

Southeast Georgia ranks high on the list of top regions for lightning strikes in the United States, especially in the summer months. Lightning occurs in all thunderstorms, since lightning's effect on the air is the cause of thunder. The discharge of electricity in a lightning strike can easily spread in a swamp, since water is a conductor of this current. Most trees hit by lightning die immediately, as the strike travels through them and causes gases, or steam, to accumulate. In simple terms, the tree then explodes from the inside out. Lightning is a regular cause of fire in the

Okefenokee. A related factor that influences these ignitions is constant evaporation in the swamp, which leads, especially during summers, to the formation of more rainstorms, many with lightning. Due to climate change, droughts are becoming more frequent than they were in the past, and lightning storms have also increased in frequency, leading to shorter periods between fires.

Fortunately, the Fish and Wildlife Service and the National Wildlife Refuge now work alongside nature to ensure a regular sequence of managed fires on the uplands surrounding the swamp (fires in ONWR are allowed to burn). Prescribed fires keep this vegetation in check in the way that lightning-caused fires have in the past. ONWR manages prescribed burns on about six thousand to ten thousand acres of uplands annually. In addition, with lower understory vegetation in the uplands, it is easier to prevent beneficial wildfires within the National Wildlife Refuge from moving beyond its boundaries. This allows animals and plants to continue to prosper while sparing people's homes. This does not mean that naturally occurring fires may not become

Ben and Harry Chesser at Gap o' Grand Prairie, viewed from the north, with smoke drifting across from a burning bay (Francis Harper, 1932). The Chessers lived in the swamp. *Francis Harper, Zach S. Henderson Library Special Collections, Georgia Southern University.*

A sign in the Suwannee Canal. The Okefenokee is also a National Wilderness Area, its boundaries slightly different than those of the national refuge. *Larry Woodward, USFWS.*

uncontrollable or that prescribed burns will not occasionally do harm; it does mean that the Okefenokee is healthier than it would be otherwise.

Before we understood the importance of prescribed burning, federal and state government workers and the public in general often assumed that fire was malicious and something to prevent or stomp out at all costs. This is understandable, given that ONWR, for example, was open to visitors who may be careless with fire, whether from a lighter or matches. Those alive in the 1960s and 1970s remember the national campaign by the Forest Service starring "Smokey the Bear," whose image appeared in commercials and advertisements that warned about the negative effect of fire on wildlife. Smokey's motto was, "Only *you* can prevent forest fires." Now, however, we recognize the importance of fire and its existence alongside drought and periods of rain in the Okefenokee.[11]

PART II

HISTORY

4

INDIGENOUS AMERICANS AND EUROPEAN SETTLERS

In the late 1700s, the natural historian and explorer William Bartram traveled extensively through the Southeast, including southern Georgia. In his memoir of this four-year voyage, *Travels through North and South Carolina, Georgia, East and West Florida, the Cherokee Country, the Extensive Territories of the Muscogulgees, or Creek Confederacy, and the Country of the Chactaws*, Bartram briefly described the "Ouaquaphenogaw" and its islands, although he does not seem to have entered the swamp himself. Relying on local Muscogee (Creek) Natives for information, he related:

> *The present generation of Creeks represent* [one of the swamp's islands] *to be a most blissful spot of the earth: they say it is inhabited by a peculiar race of Indians, whose women are incomparably beautiful; they also tell you that this terrestrial paradise has been seen by some of their enterprising hunters, when in pursuit of game, who being lost in inextricable swamps and bogs, and on the point of perishing, were unexpectedly relieved by a company of beautiful women, whom they call daughters of the sun, who kindly gave them provisions.*[12]

The hunters were saved by the mysterious women but were still unable to reach the island: "In their endeavors to approach it, they were involved in perpetual labyrinths, and, like enchanted land, still as they imagined they had just gained it, it seemed to fly before them, alternately appearing and disappearing."[13] Afterward, they were "never…able again to find that enchanting spot, nor even any road or pathway to it."[14] They did, however, come across footprints and other signs of its occupation.

Bartram contributed to a myth that, in various forms, appears in historical accounts and cultural representations of swamplands like the Okefenokee: they are enchanted and Edenic places that are magically resistant to penetration by outsiders, home to unusual animals and mysterious people. This type of legend predates Bartram, as A.H. Wright noted in his 1945 history of the swamp. In 1769, a traveler had already described,

> A great swamp, called by the Indians Ekanphaenoka or the Terrible Ground…[it] is supposed to be bottomless, having been found impassible by all who ever attempted to cross it.…The Indians (from an ancient tradition) have a notion that it is inhabited by a race of immortals, which they call the ESTE EATCHASIKKO or invisible people of whom they tell many marvelous and absurd Stories.[15]

Finally, a source from 1819 tells us, "The warlike Indians of the Creeks and Seminoles have a religious veneration for this immense desert; they say it is inhabited by aerial beings, who interdict the intrusion of man."[16] The Muscogee were fearful of venturing into the swamp at night due to these ethereal beings, the source goes on to say, and this fear formed part of their "superstitious veneration."

Today, visitors to the swamp follow official maps and are guided by expert naturalists, not mysterious daughters of the sun or invisible beings. The Okefenokee has, however, been inhabited by humans for quite some time. Trail Ridge was eventually used by Native people as a travel route, connecting present-day northeast Florida and southeast Georgia. As flora and fauna proliferated in the Okefenokee, humans who traveled this route or lived in the surrounding areas were drawn to the swamp as a seasonal hunting site. During the Woodland period (1000 BCE to 1000 CE), the Deptford, Swift Creek and Weeden Island cultures appeared in succession. These cultures were less nomadic than earlier ones, and hunting camps were established on the hammocks and islands of the Okefenokee. Chris Trowell describes how a few villages, particularly on Chesser Island, were maintained during the Weeden Island period; Floyds, Cowhouse, Billys and Blackjack Islands were also inhabited. Artifacts from the era include projectile points and pottery shards. Conch shells found in the Okefenokee are, moreover, evidence that inhabitants of these villages traded with other groups along the Atlantic coast. After the Weeden Culture diminished,

A Native mound in the Okefenokee. *Chris Trowell.*

a Savannah Culture (1200–1650 CE) emerged, sometimes at the sites of previous villages.[17]

The Wheedon Island people and the Hitichiti and Timucua cultures that followed were "mound builders" or "mound people," appellations given to pre-Columbian communities that built earthworks. Depending on its size, a tumulus may have served as a chief's residence, a ceremonial structure or the burial site of nobles. Okefenokee mounds are small and probably served as burial sites. At least one has been excavated, revealing a dozen or so skeletons. The mounds are protected by federal legislation and should not be disturbed.

In the early 1600s, the Spanish, who called the Okefenokee Laguna de Oconi, built missions in an effort to spread Catholicism among the Timucua, who resided in what is present-day northern Florida. A few of these missions were located near the Okefenokee at Santiago de Oconi and Ibihica. In fact, the Timucua may have migrated to the swamp area to escape the Spanish military. Overall, the Timucua developed an extensive and elaborate culture, with about thirty-five chiefdoms throughout northern Florida, some with fortifications. Their population at the time of the arrival of the Spanish, with whom they were initially friendly, has been estimated at two hundred thousand. By the early 1800s, however, the Timucua had been decimated by Europeans.

Muscogee Natives began arriving in southern Georgia from northern Georgia and South Carolina before the 1600s. Several bands formed the Creek Confederacy. The "Lower Creeks" of southern Georgia, especially the Hitchiti, used the Okefenokee as a hunting ground, and some established themselves in the area. Like the Timucua, Lower Creeks lived in villages, some with up to one hundred log homes. A *miko* was either a red chief, who ruled in time of war, or a white chief, who led the town in peacetime. At the center of each town was a round building, where meetings and ceremonies were held. Property was owned by women and inherited through the maternal line. Their significant ceremonies included the Boskita, or Green Corn Ceremony, which Antonio J. Waring has called "the most impressive ceremonial in the entire Southeast."[18] Inspired by former mound ceremonies, the Boskita included a late summer fire ceremony, during which a priest lighted the New Fire. This annual celebration of new crops helped cement a sense of belonging in a community. It lasted several days and included dances and the drinking of a special brew. During this time, women cleaned all traces of the "old fire" from their homes, while men tended to the New Fire.[19]

Returning to the Okefenokee, those who inhabited the swamp's islands were often refugees from larger events, such as the Revolutionary War, clashes between Native groups and, eventually, the Seminole Wars of the first half of the nineteenth century. The Yamasee, a group of mixed Native heritage who inhabited the coast of South Carolina and Georgia, were identified by Bartram as escapees into the swamp: "They [the Creeks Bartram met] tell another story concerning the inhabitants of [the Okefenokee]…which is, that they are the posterity of a fugitive remnant of the ancient Yamasee, who escaped massacre after a bloody and decisive conflict between them and the Creek nation…and here found an asylum, remote and secure from the fury of their proud conquerors."[20] The story is not historically accurate but does suggest how long ideas have circulated about those who sought refuge in the Okefenokee.

Benjamin Hawkins, the federal Indian agent mentioned in part I, was widely admired by Natives, and he became known as the "Beloved Man of the Four Nations." By all accounts, he was as much a defender of the Muscogee as possible against the "*E-cun-nau-nux-ulgee*: People greedily grasping after the lands of the red men," a Muscogee term he recorded.[21] Hawkins also presented a reputedly firsthand account of a refugee

Benjamin Hawkins and the Creek Natives on his plantation along the Flint River in central Georgia, circa 1805. Artist unknown. *Art Collection/ Alamy stock photograph.*

Native who lived in the Okefenokee, perhaps on Billys Island. Although it is difficult to distinguish between the Muscogee account of this and Hawkins's additions, the passage is worth citing, especially given the lack of Native voices in most historical sources:

> *Ho-ith-lepoie Tus-tun-nug-ge-thluc-co, an Indian who resided in it* [the Okefenokee] *many years, says that, "The Little St. John's* [the Suwannee] *may be ascended far into the swamp, and that it is not practicable to go far up the St. Mary's, as it loses itself in the swamp; that there is one ridge on the west side of the St. John's, and three on the east. The growth is pine, live and white oak; the soil good; the lakes abound in fish and alligators. On the ridges and in the swamps there were a great many bear, deer, and tigers." He lived on the ridge west of the St. John's, and was, with his family, very healthy. Being unwilling to take part in the war between the United States and Great Britain, he moved there to be out of the way of it, was well pleased with his situation, and should have continued to reside there, but for the beasts of prey, which destroyed his cattle and horses. He could walk around the swamp in five days.*[22]

Here, the Okefenokee is presented as a site of refuge and retreat from human violence, although not a retreat from wild animals ("tigers" probably refers to Florida panthers). We will come across this type of depiction of the swamp as a refuge or shelter again and again.

Confusion about the history of Native peoples in and around the Okefenokee is sometimes caused by confusion between the terms *Creek* and *Seminole*. In general, it is best to be wary of simplifying the nomenclature of Native groups when, in fact, the distinctions and connections among these groups are quite complex. In very general terms, though, the Muscogee of Georgia were labeled either Lower or Upper Creeks. After a civil war in 1812–13, the "Lower" Creeks, who lived in the southernmost parts of Georgia and Alabama, migrated to Florida, at first along the Panhandle and later expanding southward. These people became known as Seminoles. This name is often translated to mean "renegades" or "runaways," but Hawkins, who studied the Muscogeon language, states that it translates to "wild men." He explains in his 1848 essay, "The Creek Confederacy," "The name of Seminoles was given to them, on account of their being hunters, and attending but little to agriculture"[23] They were renegades, then, in the sense that they did not settle and plant crops. Hawkins also remarks that the Muscogee considered the Seminoles part of their nation until the United States government began to treat them as a distinct people.[24]

The encroachment of whites into the Okefenokee area led to friction with the Seminoles, who resisted displacement west of the Mississippi River along what became known as the Trail of Tears following the Indian Removal Act of 1830. This was especially true in the 1830s. At the time, the attacks of whites on Seminoles and Muscogee in general were called "raids," whereas Native attacks were called "massacres." Chris Trowell wrote, "Terror reigned in the Okefenokee area between 1836 and 1840. Murders by Indians, settlers, and troublemakers were common."[25] "Troublemakers" refers to white marauders, who are often forgotten when these difficult years are considered. One such attack occurred in 1836, when a militia murdered fourteen of a group of fifty to sixty Natives who had gathered on the west side of the Okefenokee at a site called Battle Bay. A lull in the violence followed, but it was brief. Attacks back and forth along the southern edge of the swamp in 1838, along with memories of the murder of members of the Wildes family near Waycross in 1832, led to federal involvement, which Georgia had wanted for quite a while.

Forts, some from late in the 1700s, were refitted, and new ones were built. Fort Alert had been constructed in 1812 at a trading post along the St. Marys River called Trader's Hill. During much of the nineteenth century, this was the local place to shop, worship, transport goods and find the sheriff. One of fifteen or so outposts built on the rim around the Okefenokee for the purpose of apprehending resistant Natives, Fort Alert was rebuilt as Fort Henderson, which, soon enough, was renamed Fort Jackson. Other forts included Forts Dearborn, Mudge and Floyd. These perimeter forts and the growth of Trader's Hill indicate that the number of white settlers around and even within the swamp was increasing. Incidentally, Trader's Hill became the seat

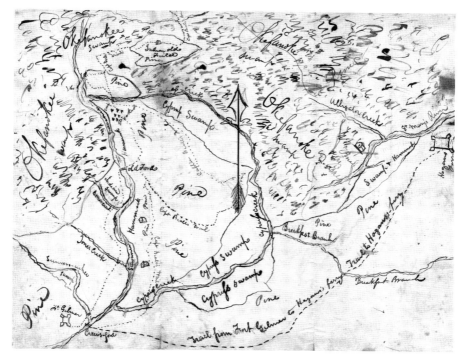

A handwritten manuscript map of the seat of the Second Seminole War in the Okefenokee region. The map is believed to have been created by Major Greenleaf Dearborn, a commanding officer who participated in General Charles Rinaldo Floyd's campaign through the region in November 1838. The map's primary feature is the location of a number of named and unnamed forts surrounding the Okefenokee Swamp and the location of the route of Captain Benjamin Lloyd Beall and his detachment of soldiers in September 1838. Second Seminole War, Okefenokee Region Manuscript Map *(1837/38) Greenleaf Dearborn, Hargrett Rare Book and Manuscript Library, University of Georgia.*

of Charlton County in 1854. In 1901, however, the seat was moved to the newer town of Folkston, following the arrival of the railroad, which replaced the river as the preferred mode of transportation for merchandise and, as a result, led to the depopulation of Trader's Hill.

Finally, General Charles Rinaldo Floyd was dispatched by the state to quell the violence once and for all. His father, General John Floyd, had established the family plantation in Camden Country, served in the state legislature and led troops against the Muscogee in the Battles of Autossee (1813) and Calebee Creek (1814). Charles Rinaldo inherited the plantation and was also a state legislator. He had led the removal of the Cherokee from northern Georgia in 1830, so it was natural that he was assigned to force the Seminole from the Okefenokee area. He thus became the leader of the

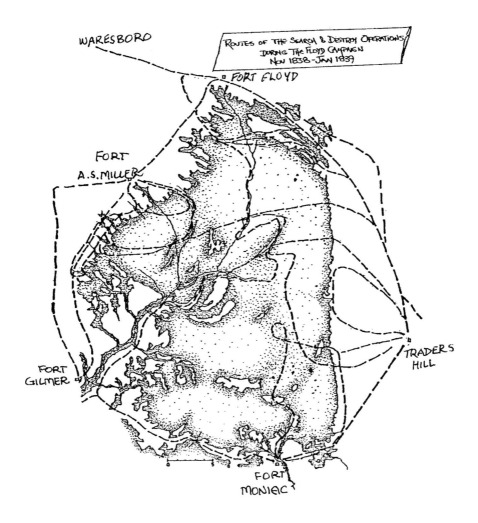

Forts in the Okefenokee Rim during the Seminole Wars. *Chris Trowell.*

militia campaign organized under President Andrew Jackson to push the "Five Civilized Nations" (the Cherokee, Chickasaw, Choctaw, Creek and Seminole) westward. Most Seminole and other Muscogee were "relocated" by the mid-1840s, with a few hundred Seminole leaving for southwest Florida, where their descendants remain. But this complicated process was completed only after the Second Seminole War (1835–42).

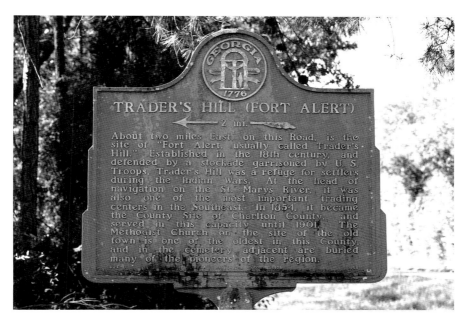

Trader's Hill Historical Marker. *Larry Woodward, USFWS.*

In 1838, Floyd and his men arrived at an abandoned island that was known as Chepuky; the village on it was called Chepucky-tolo-fa. This is assumed to be Billys Island, which had been inhabited long before the arrival of the Seminoles. The island is one of the largest islands in the swamp, and it will come up again in this book. Floyd set up a temporary fort on Billys Island, Fort Walker, and burned what remained of the Native homes there. He and his 230 or so men then set out to burn another Native village, this one on Floyds Island, where an estimated 30 Seminoles were living. In fact, the village had been abandoned two months before their arrival. Still, Floyd's men built a blockhouse and burned what remained of the structures. He described this in his diary entry for November 13, 1838:

> *For 8½ hours we struggled through one of the most formidable swamps in the world, sometimes waist deep in mud & water, & reached the famed Island, never before seen by white man. It is indeed a most beautiful place,—high & dry, with magnificent oak & laurel trees. Discovered a large Indian Camp, an Indian town with 14 or 15 very comfortable houses—but no Indians. By the signs, they had left the Island about 2 months, & were in number about 150. Camped in a beautiful hammock. My officers named the Island "Floyd's Island"—by which it will hereafter be known.[26]*

Floyd left the Okefenokee in March 1839 and returned to his plantation, his reputation as an overly strict disciplinarian having made it difficult for him to continue leading men. Major Charles Nelson assumed his role. A few years later, after a few Native raids in the southern part of the swamp at Soldiers Camp Island, the Okefenokee rim forts, including Fort Jackson at Trader's Hill, were closed, and the Army patrols were disbanded. The Second Seminole War was over.[27]

General Floyd noted repeatedly in his diary that the Okefenokee was a harsh land; his and his men's march through it has been remembered as the first time white men traversed the swamp completely, but their journey was an incredible slog. The foreboding nature of the swamp, combined with the forts that had been established in its vicinity, worked to deny its status as a haven during the war and the years surrounding it. A December 1841 letter written by an Army representative to Governor Charles James McDonald of Georgia about the routes into the swamp from Florida used by the Seminoles is worth reading in full:

> *There are two routes by which the marauding parties of Indians from Florida approach the swamp, the eastern route, by Kingsley's pond and New River, passes near Fort Moniac; the western by the natural bridge of the Santa Fe and up per Suwannee, passes near Fort Gilmer. These routes are dictated by the nature of the country.…While Forts Moniac and Gilmer have been occupied, the Indians have generally desisted from deprivations in the vicinity of the swamp.…These facts show the great importance of the two positions, which may be regarded as the keys of the swamp; and their adequacy, with active garrisons, to afford competent protection to the Okefenokee frontier.*[28]

In a letter to the War Department from March 1842, however, Governor McDonald strongly insists that there are still Seminoles in the area and, in addition, that the troops posted there are not in any way capable of diminishing this threat: "Those stationed for the protection of the country, instead of discharging their duty, are almost as troublesome as the savages in the work of murder and destruction of property. I have taken the defense of the state into my own hands."[29] This letter underscores that the early 1840s continued to be troubling times for settlers on the Okefenokee rim, due to problems within the military as well as occasional Native incursions. The back-and-forth about whether there were still Natives in the area soon came to an end, however.

Cultural historian Megan Kate Nelson has summarized the end of the Second Seminole War:

> *As Seminoles retreated from the Okefenokee hinterlands after 1842 and migrated to southern Florida, Georgia and Florida businessmen and politicians began to focus on the Okefenokee as a site of land development. Charles Floyd's traverse of the swamp and his written accounts of the "great monster"* [Floyd's term for the Okefenokee] *and its potential whetted their appetites.*[30]

We will see in the next chapter how white settlers' appetites for the expansion of the American ideal into the swamp led to drainage attempts and widespread logging, impoverishing some men while enriching others, and ultimately leading in the second and third decades of the twentieth century to a changed vision for what the Okefenokee could be.

SWAMP FOLLY AND CYPRESS KING

In the last decades of the nineteenth century, both local and outsider businessmen and politicians made efforts to capitalize on the Okefenokee. Repeatedly, these businessmen and politicians drew up plans for either pacifying the swamp by cutting through it on the way to making money elsewhere or transforming the quivering earth into land that would itself turn a profit. But first, that land had to be localized and quantified. Given that a chunk of the swamp juts into Florida just to the west of the first miles of the St. Marys River, the process of demarcating the Georgia-Florida state border involved the Okefenokee. Andrew Ellicott, acting for the United States, and Stephen Minor, acting for Spain, began an expedition into the Okefenokee in 1799 with the goal of establishing just such a clear boundary. A long succession of surveys of the Okefenokee followed, many of them unfinished. Ellicott did not complete his survey, but he did place a state boundary stone at the headwaters of the St. Marys at what is called Ellicott's Mound. This did not settle matters, however.[31]

The United States purchased Florida from Spain in 1819, and a new succession of surveyors entered the swamp, only to be interrupted in their attempts by the Seminole Wars. When Florida became a state in 1845, boundary disputes were revived. In 1854, the federal government ordered Georgia and Florida to conduct a final survey. Alexander Allen represented Georgia and, along with Benjamin F. Whitner, the Florida representative, scouted the southern swamp for a month before disagreements led to another failed endeavor. Allen did, however, leave a captivating record of

Ellicott's Mound at the headwaters of the St. Marys River, marking the boundary line between Georgia and Florida. *Michael Lusk, USFWS.*

his impressions of the swamp. His frustrations and genuine fears in the Okefenokee are expressed in the following excerpts, taken from various parts of his journal:

> *The scene is indescribable. Thick and boggy, peats of land of large extent present themselves everywhere....It is exceedingly hot and I almost faint* [it is June]....*These places certainly are the gloomiest spots on*

Ellicott's Mound
Historical Marker.
Michael Lusk, USFWS.

earth....We press on getting tired and hot and some take snake bite....
We could hear [alligators] *roaring all day, at one time like distant*
thunder and then like the bellowing of a bull....Thousands of all kinds
of birds are to be seen....The air is fowl with [birds'] *cries for fear we*
would disturb their young. The flock is so numerous, as to make the place
exceedingly offensive.[32]

Such descriptions resemble how General Floyd would describe his time
spent in the Okefenokee fifteen years earlier.

The desire for a commercial waterway from the Atlantic Ocean to
the Gulf of Mexico, traversing Georgia and Florida, formed part of a
wider movement in the United States. In the late eighteenth and early
nineteenth centuries, industry and government favored the construction
of long transport canals, including the Ohio and Erie and Wabash and
Erie Canals. The major goal of these canals was to facilitate the movement
of merchandise in the days before railroads crisscrossed the nation. A
waterway linking the ocean and gulf was a no-brainer to industrialists and
politicians. It would save time (and thus money), and it had the added
benefit of allowing ships headed from the East Coast to ports along the
Gulf of Mexico to avoid the dangerous waters around the southern tip

of Florida. Such a canal could begin at the St. Johns River in northern Florida or even at the St. Marys River and then empty into the Gulf of Mexico or one of the rivers flowing into it, such as the Suwannee.

None of these efforts got off the ground, however. Then, a mid-century proposal in the Georgia legislature ordered a survey to be done in 1856–57 by Richard L. Hunter. The goal this time was to build canals—but not for their own sake. Instead, canals would lead to the drainage of the swamp, yielding dry land fit for agriculture. But again, this plan went nowhere, and a similar plan in the mid-1870s (the Q.A. Gilmore Report) also never took off.[33] Still, leaving potential farmland fallow annoyed many in Georgia. One legislator summed up what others were thinking: "[The Okefenokee is] a land of Egypt, a Goshen, for corn and wine and oil and sugar cane and sweet potatoes.…If you drain it, it will quit shaking, and stand as firm as the everlasting mountains."[34] "If you drain it, it will quit shaking" was, in effect, the unspoken rally cry for subsequent attempts to alter the hydrology of the Okefenokee. It was imperative, some argued, to recuperate "America's Greatest Trackless Waste" (waste of land, that is) in the words of newspaperman Lloyd A. Wilhoit.[35] Although the state had decided in 1866 to donate the land to the Georgia Orphan's Home, which could sell off the worthless land and benefit from the resulting small profit, by the 1880s, there was enough confidence in the drainage idea to reverse this decision.

In the Industrial Age, companies formed and dissolved at lightning speed, and this was true of more than one drainage company that formed with the Okefenokee in mind. The 1881 sale of 4 million acres of the Florida Everglades by the State of Florida to a Philadelphia tycoon investor surely had an influence on the desire to form an Okefenokee company. The benefits of swamp drainage, as understood at the time, would include the creation of usable, taxable land that would contribute to efforts to bring Georgia into the modern industrial and agricultural era. The Okefenokee was a centerpiece of this desire. Among the investors in the Okefenokee Land and Drainage Company, formed in 1889, was Frank Clingman Folks, a doctor and the son of William Branden Folks, the namesake of the town of Folkston and a founder of Waycross. F.C. Folks was, in fact, the senator who introduced the bill to create this company. Local resident Laura Walker Singleton later used an interesting descriptor of the Okefenokee to describe this bill: "It was while Dr. Folks was a member of the Georgia Senate that he introduced a bill to sell the state-owned Okefenokee Swamp, one of the largest and densest freaks of nature known to mankind."[36] The sale price of the swamp provoked heated debate in the legislature and newspapers; in the end, bids were made, and Folks's group won, ultimately buying 235,000 acres for $0.26½ cents per acre.

Still, the dubious honor of being the first to truly attempt to drain the swamp goes not to Folks, whose company did not meet the legislature's requirements, but to Henry R. Jackson, a successful Atlanta lawyer whose manipulation of the swamp came to be derided as "Jackson's Folly." The Suwanee Canal Company (with Suwannee spelled with one "n") incorporated in 1890, with Jackson as president.[37] It successfully produced a survey and began its construction in the allotted time given by the legislature. Jackson's goal was two-pronged. A ditch, which would begin where the National Wildlife Refuge buildings are now located, would head east out of the swamp and drain the wetland into the St. Marys River; from there, it would drain into the Atlantic. A wider canal, heading west from the dock at ONWR, would facilitate the drainage and serve as a waterway for removing lumber from the interior. Visitors today can see part of what remains of the folly's ditch along a marked trail, and boat tours travel along what Jackson completed of his canal, the Suwannee Canal, which is maintained as a waterway into the Okefenokee interior.

Using a family first name, Jackson called the site where he set up operations Camp Cornelia. By 1891, work on the drainage ditch to Cowhouse Creek, a small tributary of the St. Marys River, was underway. Jackson did not fully appreciate, however, the obstacle posed by a remnant of the formation of the swamp thousands of years before: the ancient barrier island of Trail Ridge, which spread up to two miles wide and rose up to thirty-five feet above the water level of the swamp. Trail Ridge ensures that waters to its

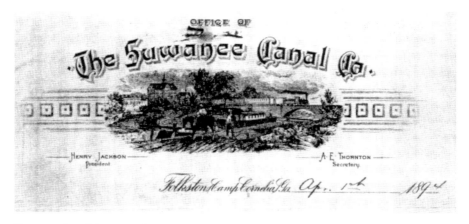

Suwanee Canal Company letterhead, 1894. *Public domain.*

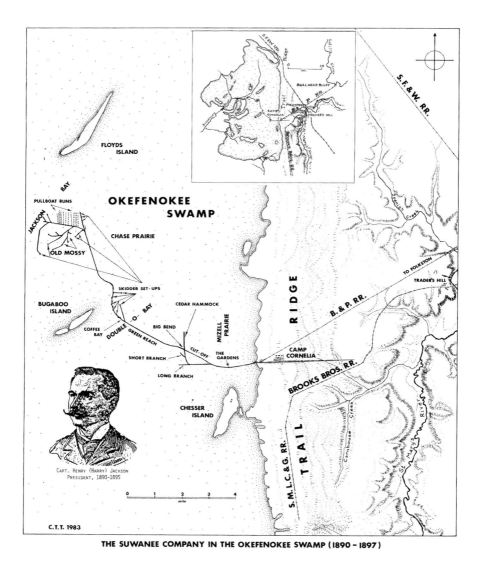

THE SUWANEE COMPANY IN THE OKEFENOKEE SWAMP (1890 – 1897)

The Suwanee Canal Company in the Okefenokee Swamp, 1890–97. *Chris Trowell.*

west flow eventually into the Gulf of Mexico, a flow that cannot be reversed. Cutting into Trail Ridge also revealed unanticipated water springs—more and more water that would need to be channeled. Jackson nevertheless pursued his passion, first with convict labor digging with their hands and later with miners using hydraulic pumps drawn by horses to dig through Trail Ridge. On the canal to the west, which was to be forty-five feet wide and six feet deep, a paddlewheel steamboat hauled timber out after powered dipper dredges cut through the peat.

By 1894, the Suwanee Canal Company was focused on lumbering instead of drainage, at first as a means of financing the drainage but then as an end in itself. A pine lumber sawmill had been built at Camp Cornelia; now, Jackson wanted a cypress sawmill, which would be more costly. Timber was removed from the Okefenokee and carried by the steamboat *Cornelia* to the sawmill; the sawn lumber was then transported by an elevated narrow-gauge rail line to Folkston. Beginning in 1895–96, an overhead steam skidder, the latest lumbering technology, was employed following the success of this machine in North Carolina swamps. Logs were carried on pull boats like those used in Louisiana bayous. These aided operations, but novel technologies did not come cheap. Rail freight costs were also high. Jackson's company could never get ahead of the game due to transportation costs. Drainage had been one thing, but logging with the new industrial methods was another. Jackson continued to make poor financial decisions, and the company was further hampered by the fact that the desired timber was farther into the swamp from where the canal had been dug, requiring more canal construction deeper into the Okefenokee.

The Suwannee Canal, looking east. *Larry Woodward, USFWS.*

When Jackson died unexpectedly in 1895 after an appendectomy, millions of feet of unsold board timber remained around Camp Cornelia. He had lost about $1 million in the Suwanee Canal Company. His elderly father, also named Henry R. Jackson, became president of the company and endeavored to continue the quixotic effort, but he did not prove to be a more astute businessperson. After he died, the acres were sold in 1901 to Philadelphia capitalist Charles Hebard and his two sons, Charles S. and Daniel L. The price for the land was $175,000. Henry Jackson, the son, as others before him, was thwarted by the elusive hydrology of the Okefenokee.

At the turn of the century, Henry B. Plant and Henry Flagler barreled through Florida with their railroads, opening the South in ways that took industry by storm. In and around the Okefenokee, the railroad became the key factor in successfully hauling lumber and other products out and sending them to where they were transformed into merchandise that was sold the world over. Though some local drainage was necessary for timbering, Charles Hebard did not want or need to drain the swamp. This, combined with the promise of the railroad, ensured that the new Okefenokee profiteer would not fail. In the end, five hundred miles of railroad were built in the Okefenokee. This was temporary rail, as the tracks that were previously used to extend one way into areas ripe for timber removal were pulled up and re-laid to extend in new directions.

Water was no longer of interest, whether it quivered or not; it was rail that sped up the swamp's lumber industry. Will Cox, a longtime worker in the swamp in the twentieth century, said, "We went after the cypress and cut down three thousand acres of trees. I was a part of all that. We didn't know any better."[38] Along with several other companies—but none as dominant—the Hebard Cypress Company removed almost all of the Okefenokee's old-growth timber, in particular the pond cypress, selling it worldwide for the construction of homes, other structures and furniture. In addition, by about 1900, timbering had decimated the longleaf pine that characterized the rim of the Okefenokee. The end of lumbering in the swamp finally came in the late 1920s, due in part to a cultural and political shift from a desire to reap mass profits from the wetland to a desire to conserve it. By then, there was basically nothing left to remove.[39]

When the Charles Hebard and Sons Company purchased almost 250,000 acres of the Okefenokee from the Jackson family trust in 1901, the company's namesake was already established as a lumber baron. Since the 1880s, Charles Hebard had been at work deforesting land along Lake Superior in northern Michigan. Born in Connecticut, Hebard moved to Philadelphia,

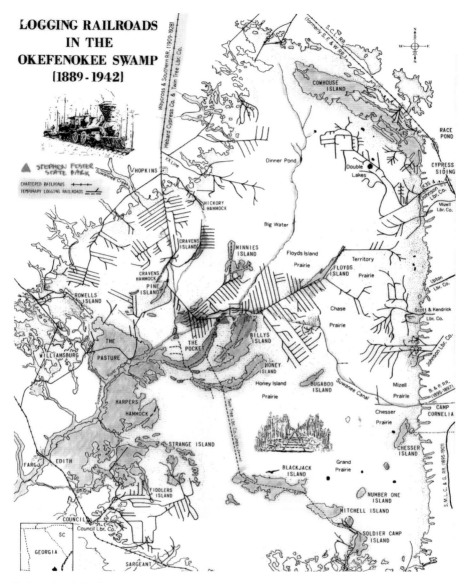

Railroads of the Okefenokee, 1889–1942. *C.T. Trowell, 1995.*

where many industrial barons—some of whom had already been involved in land deals in Florida and Georgia—lived. Hebard's death at the age of seventy-one in 1902 caused delays, but these did not ultimately impede his sons from continuing their father's goals. The Hebard family eventually owned around 300,000 acres of the Okefenokee and was responsible for removing over 430 million board feet of timber from it, dwarfing by a huge amount the Suwanee Canal Company's 11 million board feet.

Hebard invested $2 million in his venture, considerably more than Jackson could raise. And unlike the changing goals that dogged the Suwanee Canal Company, Hebard's enterprise was single-mindedly fixated on lumber. Turpentining and other swamp-related industries (which will be discussed later) were done on land leased to other companies, but cypress was king for Hebard and Hebard was the cypress king. He and his sons knew the business and hired experienced lumbermen from Michigan and other northern states. After Charles Sr.'s death, several years were devoted to careful study before the operation commenced in 1909 in the western half of the Okefenokee. An area near Waycross (and now part of it) became the site of Hebardville, a short-lived bustling mill town linked to the swamp by railroad. John Hopkins, the company superintendent agent, managed the business down to the smallest details. Pine Plume Lumber managed marketing for Hebard Cypress, which was to become a premier timber board outfit. The swamp had, finally, become useful.

Charles Sr. had originally hired Hopkins, a lawyer and civil engineer from Darien, Georgia, to do a timber survey of the area. Hamp Mizell, a local Swamper, helped draw the survey lines, which progressed one mile per day according to Hopkins's memoir, *Forty-Five Years with the Okefenokee Swamp*. Hopkins was not familiar with the swamp before his arrival to work for Hebard, but he quickly fell head over heels for it. It may seem odd that although Hopkins was the brains behind most of the Hebard commercial success in deforesting the Okefenokee, he also became the first manager of ONWR and worked diligently in conservation. From the first page of his memoir, he noted that his work over the long years resembled a "mothering" of the Okefenokee.[40] In his conclusion, Hopkins wrote that during his eight years at the National Wildlife Refuge he was engaged in repairing the damage he had caused working for Hebard. Perhaps the former superintendent agent of Hebard Cypress considered his time as a conservationist to be penance. Turning back now to the first decades of the twentieth century, we should keep in mind the complexity of this man's engagement with the swamp and how it represents shifting views on the value of wilderness in the United States.

Charles Jr. and Daniel Hebard established the Hebard Lumber Company in 1904. Hebard Lumber leased just under 220,000 acres to Hebard Cypress, founded in 1907, and Hopkins was appointed general superintendent of the latter. As such, he headed up the construction of Hebardville. From 1909 to 1927, this was a large company community with about 3,500 inhabitants, including employees and their families. Logging began in earnest in 1909, and sawing began the next year. This marked the beginning of seventeen years of Hebard dominion.

Clearing the Okefenokee of cypress was a mammoth operation that proceeded slowly as the company advanced farther into the "dense jungle." The time involved in cutting, curing and transporting logs to sawmills required that workers be on site daily, and many lived on the edge of the Okefenokee. The hamlet of Hopkins, planned by and named for the superintendent, was set up twenty miles south of Waycross, just outside the northwest area of the Okefenokee, on what became known as Swamp Road (today, this road leads to the Okefenokee Swamp Park). A railroad was constructed to link the Hopkins mill to the Hebardville mill; Hebard Lumber Company owned this railroad, called the Waycross and Southern Railroad.

Meanwhile, a system for expanding a temporary network of spur tram rails in the swamp was established. Using steam-powered pile drivers and Lidgerwood overhead skidders, tracks were attached to pilings that stretched deep into the peat. The skidders then piled logs by the rail tracks, and American loader cranes placed them in rail cars. The first logs were on their way to Hebardville in late 1909, and in time, forty railcars per day made the trip. From there, they went by railroad to Savannah, the port from which Hebard lumber was sent into the world.

Steam engine skidders, also called steam donkeys, were commonplace in the timber industry by 1900, having replaced cross-cut saws and wagons drawn by animals. Skidders were a more efficient and economic means of removing timber. They caused a staggering amount of destruction where they were used, however, and not only to the specific trees uprooted and removed. The pernicious process on Billys Island was chronicled by an *Atlanta Constitution* journalist in 1921:

> *Early one morning, we went to a section of the swamp where logging was being done—of course we went by train; there was no other way to go— and saw the immense trunks of the cypress being hurled about and handled with seemingly as great ease as it they were toothpicks....Workmen* [then] *proceed into the swamp and begin felling timber, which for several months has been "girdled"* [slowly killed] *with a cut ring so that the wood will become sufficiently light to float on the water....The giants of the virgin forest, crash to earth with a groan and a terrific upheaval of muck and*

spray. The cutters, working on an average of waist deep in muck, trim them, and they are ready for loading…the signal is given, the big steam engine pants and conquers, and [the] *monarch of the forest, which for years untold has looked down upon the teeming wild life of the swamp, is swung high into the air and crashes through the path cleared to the waiting flatcar.…I was told that the average cutting of logs was fifty cars per day, or about 300 logs.…If the Hebard company continues cutting at its present rate, it is estimated that the cypress timber supply will be exhausted in about eight years.*[41]

These observations suggest the violence and pollution associated with industrial lumbering in the early twentieth century. One can only imagine the effect this had on the alligators, spiders, orchids and vines that depended on the Okefenokee.

Just as Hebardville was a self-sufficient town with lodging, churches, schools and stores for workers and their families, a (smaller) community for logging families was established on the 3,140-acre Billys Island. Planned by John Hopkins in 1917–18, the community of about six hundred had homes along with a movie house (one of the first in Georgia), a boardinghouse, a

Honey Island Cut-Over Pine Barrens, a typical scene of devastation after the loggers have finished. *Francis Harper, Zach S. Henderson Library Special Collections, Georgia Southern University.*

barbershop, blacksmiths, a general store, taverns and even telephone lines, which ran along the railroad tracks. The railroad reached Billys by way of Jones Island, where the Stephen C. Foster State Park facilities are now located. Since Hebard and Twin Trees Lumber, which did lumbering and turpentining on the island, hired Black workers as well as white ones, there were separate churches, schools and lodgings for Black and white families. When there, Hopkins lived in a refurbished train car on Mixons Hammock, close to Billys Island.

Logging on and around Billys Island was completed within two years, at which point operations shifted to Floyds Island. The Hebards controlled only about half of the swamp's acres, and other companies had begun clearing out the rest of the Okefenokee during these years. Despite the initial thoughts of investors that the trees in the Okefenokee would go on forever, the usable cypress of the swamp was all but completely harvested, and a depression was about to hit the housing market in the United States, affecting timber companies. Billys Island was abandoned in 1926, and the employees who had lived there moved to other logging camps, most located between Hebardville and Hopkins. Hebard Lumber continued to lease some areas to small lumber businesses, but most of the rail tracks were

Billys Island, old machinery. *Larry Woodward, USFWS.*

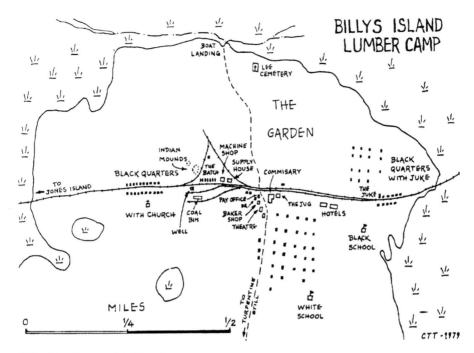

Billys Island map. *Chris Trowell.*

pulled up. (There were also logging camps at Toledo, Moniac, Council and Fargo.)

The Hebardville sawmill closed in 1927. Daniel Hebard had built a cabin on Floyds Island in 1925 specifically for winter duck hunting, leaving that railroad spur intact to accommodate the well-to-do friends he invited to hunt and fish with him. (The cabin still stands and has been listed in the National Register of Historic Places since 1999.) Hebard and his acquaintances used the lodge only from time to time, leaving a full-time caretaker on Floyds Island, Billy Spaulding, who lived there alone in a separate structure from 1925 to 1937. The Hebards still owned much of the Okefenokee, but duck hunting was their interest now, not turning a profit.

Lumbering and other industries involving trees took place outside of the swamp as well as inside it, of course. The number of mills at Fargo in the early twentieth century indicate the many products that pine, especially, offered: lumber, turpentine, pulpwood and wood chip mills made Fargo quite the bustling town at that time. Board lumber was also made into roof shingles, and resin from pine bark was turned into pitch that was used to seal cracks in boats. Companies used every piece of a tree they could

Billys Island dock. *Larry Woodward, USFWS.*

Jackson Lee with his family and relatives, Billys Island. *Kenneth Spencer Research Library, University of Kansas.*

A Black logging crew on a flat car going from Billys Island to Billy's Bay (1921). *Francis Harper, Zach S. Henderson Library Special Collections, Georgia Southern University.*

Hebard cabin on Floyds Island. *Michael Lusk, USFWS.*

to profit from the swamp, and homeowners on the East Coast and other places around the world knew the value of these products.

Pine trees did double duty: they were tapped for their resin before they were felled for lumber. The turpentine trade from pine, which involved the distillation of this resin, was second only to the business of lumbering cypress as focal points of industry in the Okefenokee in the early twentieth century. Hebard Lumber leased areas of pine trees to Twin Trees Lumber and other smaller timber companies; these companies may have also owned their own areas of the swamp. Twin Trees, for example, allowed an Alabama company, Darling Turpentine, to lease a portion of its acres on Billys Island. Darling Turpentine built a still and living quarters for workers on Billys. There was also a turpentine camp in the settlement of Toledo on the rim of the Okefenokee between Folkston and St. George with a commissary and lodging for workers, both white and Black. It appears that John Hopkins, Hebard's superintendent, also ran a turpentine camp near Camp Cornelia in the early 1930s, after Hebard left.

The collection of turpentine from longleaf, loblolly and slash pines does not kill the trees, although the resulting slash marks, still visible on trees in the swamp and its uplands, does damage them. To harvest resin (also called tar or gum), long-blade axes made the slashes. At first, a dip paddle was used to scoop out the resin, but in time, clay pots and buckets were attached to the trees to catch the product. Copper stills transformed the resin into turpentine, a product that was sent by railroad out of the swamp and to commercial enterprises. In an entry to his notebook from 1929, Francis Harper remarked the following after seeing scarred trees in the Okefenokee, "Out along canal from Camp Cordelia. New peace comes to my soul in these fair bits of prairie, tiny as they are....Away from the turpentine-scarred piney woods."[42]

Turpentine farms, as well as lumber mills, attracted Black workers. Historian W. Fitzhugh Brundage wrote that between 1870 and 1900, "the stream of black laborers and farmers increased the black population in South Georgia, from 63,421 to 208,513."[43] In reference to Ware County, he stated:

> *Employment in lumber yards and turpentine orchards required few skills but generally paid higher wages than agricultural labor. Moreover, many black laborers, especially turpentine hands, enjoyed the companionship of a largely black community of fellow workers. The attributes that made turpentining attractive to blacks, however, also made it unsettling to many whites, who complained that black turpentine hands posed a continual*

Turpentine "chipper" and slashed tree near Homerville, Georgia, 1937. *Dorothea Lange, Library of Congress Prints and Photographs Division, FSA/OWI Collection.*

threat to the social peace. Even in the best of times, many whites viewed black woodsmen with suspicion and hostility.[44]

The fear of violence in turpentine camps was ever-present due to disputes between mill owners, who aimed to control Black workers, and workers who were bent on resisting exploitation.[45]

In addition to turpentine, crosstie production (beams laid under rail tracks) was a significant enterprise in the Okefenokee Swamp and rim area. Jackson's canal was used to transport, by motorboat, logs to Camp Cornelia from Bugaboo Island and Coffee Bay for crossties. At least seven hundred thousand total crossties were harvested from the Okefenokee. Peat and sphagnum moss mining were two other industries that attracted investors to the swamp rim, especially the J.H. King Company. Like other endeavors, sphagnum moss harvesting continued after the establishment of the ONWR but only outside its boundaries, unless an old lease was still in effect.

The "drainage" of timber from the Okefenokee was successful in terms of its profits and thoroughness. A handful of old-growth cypress remains in the swamp today; these trees were left behind because they were considered damaged or too young to attract profits or because there weren't enough in one area to justify operating there. Young cypress from the time and new ones have grown since, of course, but with a maximum lifespan of up to 1,200 years, it will be a very long time before visitors see old-growth cypress again. The Okefenokee remains, its hydrology essentially unharmed by water follies, but the loss of old-growth cypress is one thing that humans will surely regret for generations to come. Still, the full quote from Will Cox about this devastation includes optimistic final words:

> *We did everything we could to destroy it. We skinned alligators until we like to drove every last one off. We killed bears, otters, foxes, and almost got rid of them. We went after the cypress and cut down three thousand acres of trees. I was a part of all that. We didn't know any better.*
>
> *But the old swamp came back. The animals came back. The trees came back. You wouldn't know where the trees were cut.*
>
> *The Okefenokee is God's work. Man couldn't destroy it, and now it is as beautiful as it ever was. It is the most beautiful place on earth. I will do everything I can to make sure it stays that way for as long as the world lasts.*[46]

6

SWAMPERS

While Hebard Lumber and other companies removed trees from the Okefenokee, Swampers, who sometimes worked for them, continued hunting and fishing as they had before, providing food for their families and selling furs and alligator skins. White settlers had been setting up homesteads in the Okefenokee area since the early 1800s, and by the 1850s, a few families had moved onto islands in the swamp proper. Historically, the distinction between those living in the swamp and those living on its rim or edge is significant, but all these inhabitants were and, at times, continue to be referred to as Swampers. As in all communities, a particular history and culture is associated with them. These farmers and hunters, mostly poor, belong to the larger category of "Crackers," or settlers of English and Scottish descent who migrated to Georgia from Virginia and the Carolinas. While landscape is always a factor in the development of a subculture, it is especially true of a place like the Okefenokee, where the presence of ever-trembling land provides, ironically, a stable foundation for a unique culture.

Visitors to cemeteries in the Okefenokee rim quickly become familiar with common Swamper family names. They include but are not limited to Barber, Carter, Chesser, Cox, Crews, Griffis, Harrison, Hendrix, Hickox, Johns, Lee, Mixon, Mizell, Roddenberry, Spaulding and Tatum. Intermarriage between the families was common, leading to various combinations of names when a woman's birth name was retained as a middle name. In the following chapter, four families are presented: the Chessers, Mizells, Mixons and

Lees. Following this, two memorable individuals who became known as the "King" and "Queen" of the Okefenokee are introduced.

Francis Harper, an important source on Swamper culture during the first decades of the twentieth century, has already been mentioned. This naturalist turned amateur folklorist came to know and respect Swampers and even lived as one himself within the Okefenokee. Familiarity with his work is essential for developing a full picture of Okefenokee life, and we have Delma Presley to thank for publishing a group of Harper's observations in *Okefinokee Album*. Born in Massachusetts in 1886, Harper first came to the swamp for two and a half weeks in 1912 ahead of a team of naturalists from Cornell University. During this trip, David Lee served as his principal guide to Billys Island. Following this, a contingent from Cornell arrived, led by A.H. Wright and W.D. Funkhouser, head of Ithaca (New York) High School, joined him. Funkhouser was later criticized by Swampers for saying derogatory things about their lifestyle on Billys Island at a public presentation, but Harper was, from the beginning, taken by the generosity and intelligence of the Swampers. Cornell biological expeditions into the Okefenokee continued until 1922.

Harper returned regularly to the Okefenokee throughout the 1910s, 1920s and 1930s, recording his observations in notebooks and publishing articles about the swamp. After receiving a PhD at Cornell and then teaching for a time at Swarthmore College, he worked for various government and private research associations and centers. He married Jean Shepard, who accompanied him to the swamp with their children and was also an important promoter of the Okefenokee. Francis Harper died in North Carolina in 1972. He envisioned writing a detailed history of the naturalists and explorers John and William Bartram, but unfortunately, he did not finish this work. Interestingly, Harper's brother Roland was also a naturalist and author of the first botanical survey of the Okefenokee, making of them a pair of brothers somewhat similar to the Bartrams.

Harper and his family lived in a tent and then a cabin on Chesser Island, and they grew close to the Chessers, an early Swamper family who lived inside the Okefenokee. In the mid-1850s, William Tennyson Chesser (1812–1886) was the first of the family to establish himself on the northern half of what was called Little Cowhouse Island, a six-hundred-plus-acre island later renamed for the family. Chessers continued to inhabit the island for just over one hundred years, making them the family who lived for the longest period within the Okefenokee's boundaries. W.T.'s sons, Robert Allen (1859–1929) and Samuel Archie

(1854–1924), lived there with their wives and children. Robert Allen lived with his family in the area of the current Suwannee Recreation Area dock, and Samuel's family lived where the current Chesser homestead is located. Robert and Samuel were buried with their wives, Lizzie and Sarah, in the Sardis Primitive Baptist Church Cemetery on the edge of the Okefenokee.

Okefenokee settlers had much in common with other nineteenth-century pioneers, but their livelihoods were sculpted by the swamp ecosystem. Farming, ranching and hunting were practiced by the Chessers starting in the 1850s. The hunting of dear and alligators, for both skins and meat, was practiced widely; the family also relied on gopher tortoises and turtles, their eggs, many kinds of fish and other game for their meals. Cows, hogs and chickens were kept. Sugarcane was one of the cash crops they grew, and cane grinding was done at the homestead. Other crops planted by this family and other Swampers were corn, sweet potatoes, tobacco and rice. A hollowed cypress log was used as a well; hollowed cypresses also served to house beehives. A quote from Charles R. Pendleton, who interviewed William T. Chesser in 1875, nicely sums up the lifestyle of those who lived within the Okefenokee:

> *I have always got along. You see I can kill deer, bear, turkey, ducks, geese— can go to Seago* [Lake Seagrove] *and catch as many fish as I want; besides, as you can see, I have lots of chickens, hogs, and cattle. I get wild honey, too, occasionally, but it is not so plentiful now as it was once. You see the 'serters* [Civil War deserters] *in the war times cleaned the bees out.*[47]

This description resembles those of Francis Harper, even in the 1910s and 1920s. To add to the family income, second- and third-generation Chessers also worked for turpentine and lumber mills with the Suwanee Canal Company, Hebard Lumber and other companies. With the opening of ONWR, they also found work with the federal government.

Samuel Archie's son, Joseph Thomas "Tom" Chesser, married Iva Lee and raised a family in the new cypress and pine home he built to replace the original W.T. Chesser home. In 1927, Tom added on to this cabin, building an attached kitchen and adding two bedrooms to the two that were already there. This is the home where he and his wife, Iva, raised their eight children, and it is the home that currently stands. It was fitted with a wood-burning stove and refrigerator in the 1940s. The walls are constructed of longleaf pine and the floors of cypress. A noticeable outbuilding is

The home of Allen Chesser. *Foreground*: Ben, Allen and Vannie Chesser. *Francis Harper papers, Kenneth Spencer Research Library, University of Kansas.*

Samuel and Sarah Chesser. Photograph displayed in the Chesser homestead. *Larry Woodward, USFWS.*

The Okefinokee Swamp Around 1925

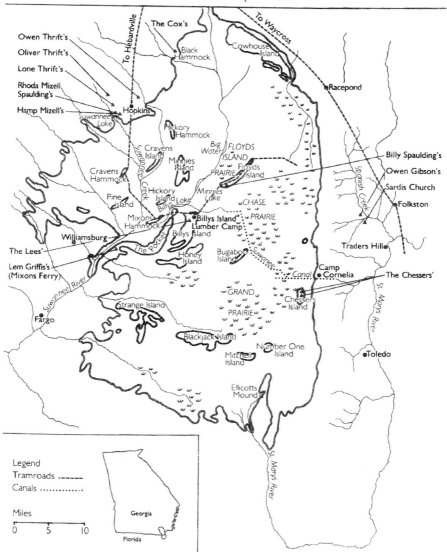

A map of the Okefenokee around 1925. *Francis Harper, Zach S. Henderson Library Special Collections, Georgia Southern University.*

the cane shed, where six to seven gallons of cane juice yielded one gallon of syrup.

In 1958, two decades after the opening of the ONWR, Iva left the homestead for Folkston, where she had been working in the lunchroom of a public school. Already in 1939, she had indicated, in letters to Jean Harper, the difficulty of maintaining the Swamper way of life on the island: "The Government are fencing us all up in the Island. I guess they intend to make it as hard for us as they can.... By them fencing the swamp down our way looks like we will have to do away with our cows," suggesting that the way of life of those living within the swamp was reaching its twilight years.[48] Once Iva left, her husband, Tom, soon gave up his stubborn resistance and joined her, purportedly due to loneliness.

Tom Chesser was the last Swamper to leave the interior of the Okefenokee behind. After he died in the early 1970s, Iva sold the homestead to ONWR for about $30,000. She then participated in its restoration by finding furniture that resembled the original pieces. (These had been moved to her new home on the edge of the Okefenokee.) In the 1970s, a Youth Conservation Corps group, under the auspices of the Fish and Wildlife Service and including at least one Chesser family member, worked to restore the homestead. But although the term *Swamper* is still used in the Okefenokee rim, the purchase of the homestead marked the end of an era. Tom and Iva were buried in the Sardis Cemetery, alongside many other Swampers.

Like the Chessers, Josiah Mizell and his wife, Martha Johns, were early settlers on the eastern edge of the swamp, probably establishing themselves near what is now called Mizell Prairie. Josiah was born in 1837; by 1860, he was a merchant in Trader's Hill. During the Civil War, he fought in Virginia with Company F of the Twenty-Sixth Regiment of the Georgia Voluntary Infantry, also known as the Okefenokee Rifles. He was captured in 1865 at

Opposite: Samuel Chesser's tombstone at Sardis Primitive Baptist Church. *Larry Woodward, USFWS.*

Above: Roxie Chesser on washday, June 1922. *Francis Harper papers, Kenneth Spencer Research Library, University of Kansas.*

Tom and Iva Chesser. Photograph displayed in Chesser homestead. *Larry Woodward, USFWS.*

Sugarcane grinding on Chesser Island. The original cane shed can be seen in the background. *Larry Woodward, USFWS.*

Josiah Mizell's tombstone at the Sardis Primitive Baptist Church Cemetery. *Larry Woodward, USFWS.*

Petersburg, Virginia, spent three months in a prison in Maryland and then walked the very long distance home to the Okefenokee. He and his wife moved to a home on Old Swamp Road near Chesser Island in the 1860s, farmed there and raised seven children. Their burial spots are also located in the Sardis Cemetery.

William Hamp Mizell, who went by "Hamp," was one of Josiah and Martha's sons and also the author, with Alexander S. McQueen, of *History of the Okefenokee Swamp* (1926). In it, Hamp Mizell asserts that his father, Josiah, was the first white man to explore the area westward from the eastern part of the Okefenokee. This was, of course, in the days before Jackson had begun to dig his canal folly. Hamp vividly described his father's trips into the Okefenokee, usually made with a neighbor, (James) Berrian Dedge. During these trips, they "discovered" what became known as Chase Prairie and Bugaboo Island. Hamp mentions that they found a Native mound on Bugaboo covered with tall pine trees, indicating for him the truth of the "claim of the Seminoles, to wit: that another race had preceded them in the Swamp."[49]

For these trips, the men loaded a small wooden boat with bacon, sweet potatoes and blankets, as well as their hunting dogs. Josiah used a long pole with a bayonet attached at the end to ward off the many alligators that threatened them; they also encountered a Florida panther. There were two ways they and other Swampers kept from becoming lost in the swamp: they observed the growth of bark on trees and the locations of eagle nests, which could be spotted from afar. After returning home, they exclaimed that the number of deer and bears on Bugaboo Island was astonishing. From that point on, Josiah and his companions added venison to their excursion stores of bacon and sweet potatoes, and hunting parties into the swamp continued regularly.

In his field notes, Harper recorded that Jack Mizell, a cousin of Hamp Mizell, took up at different times the typical jobs available around the swamp during the first half of the twentieth century. He settled at Camp Cornelia around 1929, after lumbering had mostly ceased. He worked for turpentine farms "pulling boxes" and then as a train dispatcher for the

The troubadour of the Okefenokee (Hamp Mizell) at Suwannee Lake, May 1930. *Francis Harper papers, Kenneth Spencer Research Library, University of Kansas.*

Waycross and Southern Railroad at Hopkins. His brother Tom worked at a shipyard in Brunswick, making the daily trip back and forth to the Okefenokee.

In 1852, Josiah G. Mixon homesteaded on the west side of the Okefenokee in an area soon called Mixon's Hammock. The Mixon home was located fifteen miles north of what is now Fargo and adjacent to what is now the entrance to the Stephen C. Foster State Park. The Mixons intermarried with another Swamper family, the Griffises, and the area became known as the Griffis Fish Camp in the 1930s. The camp borders the Suwannee River at its most shallow point at a crossing site that was long used by Natives and early settlers, who loaded stagecoaches on a raft to take them across the river, with the horses following. This site became known as Mixon's Ferry. The most famous of the Griffises was Lemuel, "Lem," who ran the fish camp. His son, Edwin Griffis, continues the business at the present time. There is a Mixon's Cemetery in the area of the former homestead, but the location is unmarked; the original grave markers are gone.

The Lee family was long associated with Billys Island, and several of the family's members are buried in the Lee Cemetery on the island. James Jackson Lee (1829–1888), called "Black Jim" due to his dark hair and beard, settled on the island in the late 1850s with his wife, Catherine. (John G. Crowley, by contrast, has written that Lee came to Billys Island to escape the Civil War a few years later.)[50] Charles Pendleton wrote of him:

> *Mr. Lee is almost independent of the world. The only article that he buys beside ammunition, fishing tackle and farming and mechanical implements are coffee and salt....He tans his leather and makes his own shoes, and his industrious wife and daughters spin and weave and sew up every thread of clothes they wear. He lives on government land, is lord of all he surveys, and is happy in his quiet solitude.*[51]

The Lees were the dominant Swamper family to establish themselves here, much as the Chessers occupied their island to the east. Black Jim

Britt Crews, Dave Lee and a horse and wagon, May 23, 1912. *Francis Harper papers, Kenneth Spencer Research Library, University of Kansas.*

Jackson Lee's homestead from the south. A group is standing on the porch of the house. Billys Island. *Kenneth Spencer Research Library, University of Kansas.*

built a home, raised cattle and planted sugarcane and the other typical Okefenokee crops. The Lees' cultivation of honey lead to the naming of the nearby Honey Island. Black Jim's daughter Nancy married Dan Lee, a relative, and they and other Lees continued living on Billys Island and raising families there. Dan and Nancy Lee had sons Farley, Jackson and James Harrison, who went by Harrison, and they and their families lived on Billys as long as they could. Tragically, Farley's young son, James Henry Lee, was killed on the island's railroad track by a locomotive in 1921. He is buried in the Lee Cemetery on the island, along with several other members of the family.

When Hebard left Billys Island, some Lees returned, joining those who had remained to work for the logging and turpentine companies. Various versions of how Lees, either voluntarily or only after aggressive persuasion, left the island have been recounted. According to John Hopkins, Dan and Nancy Lee were offered $1,000 by the Hebards to leave Billys Island, but they were apparently not willing to do so.[52] Hopkins further writes that all the men of the Lee families on the island worked for him, yet he was anxious to see them leave once lumbering operations were over. He recalled that the company had multiple problems with the Lees, whom he called the "natives" of Billys Island, in the period from 1926 to 1937, when the last Lee left. He seemed relieved when he wrote of Jackson Lee, for example, that "we got him out."[53]

It's worth mentioning that Hopkins also refers to two Steedleys who were living on Billys and whom he had taken to jail in Folkston when they refused to leave; he then argued for them to be released with a suspended sentence for trespassing. Hopkins even recounts that he gave one of them six dollars because he pitied their poor condition.[54] These Steedleys were most likely part of the large Steedley family established in and around Fargo in the nineteenth century. They were a Swamper family and became related to the Lees when Jemima "Minnie" Lee, the daughter of Dan and Nancy, married a Steedley. Margaret Bourke-White photographed Steedleys during the Depression, and two of the images she made appear in the book *You Have Seen Their Faces*, a photographic collection of Depression-era families first published in 1937, with captions mentioning the Okefenokee.[55] These striking photographs portray Swampers during the Depression, an extremely challenging time for people who already did not have much. In one, Lizzie Steedley nurses her baby; in the other, she and two other children, along with an elderly woman whose home she lived in, have a meal at a table. Francis Harper also referred to the family, mentioning two John Steedleys, one called Bear John and one Bread-tray John; the first was allegedly a hog thief, the second had "a hump on his chest as well as on his back."[56]

Returning to the Lees, the way certain Swampers thought of their possession of land in the Okefenokee is complicated. The Lees had been long established on the island and were understandably attached to their piece of the Okefenokee. They tried, unsuccessfully, to claim the island in court in 1901 and 1912; a 1932 effort also failed. Hebard Lumber Company controlled the land and had members of the family evicted in that year, but the circumstances of this eviction are murky. A wildfire in April 1932 damaged the remaining buildings of the old camp, but the Lees saved the boardinghouse and a few homes. Not long after, though, officials arrived and removed the family's belongings and took them to Jones Island, where the possessions were scattered, according to some. Some suspected that the fire was a result of arson, but there is no evidence of this—and it was a big fire year. In any event, the eviction was successful, and the long history of the Lees on Billys Island was all but over. Harrison Lee stayed on for a time but left in 1937, when the island was purchased from the Hebards by the government as part of the National Wildlife Refuge.[57]

This island was the most densely inhabited during the timber years and is therefore the most well-known island of the Okefenokee along with Chesser Island. That island is clearly named for the original settler family associated with it, but the origin of the name Billys Island is not clear. Drawing on Richard Hunter and M.B. Grant's survey of the swamp in 1856, Trowell states that the name probably originated during the nineteenth century, when it was first known as "Billys Old Field" for an old Native, "Indian Billy from Ware County," who lived there and was murdered in the late 1820s.[58] Trowell also proposes that this could very well be the origin of the unfounded stories of Holata Micco, called Billy Bowlegs by white settlers, a Seminole chief who would have lived on Billys Island in the mid-1800s. Wright argues, however, "There seems little evidence that these two places [Billys Island and Billy's Lake] received their names from Bowlegs, the military chief of the Seminoles and son of Cowkeeper."[59] Wright carefully delineates Billy Bowlegs's history as well as those of other men with similar-sounding names that may be the origin of the island's name. In the end, this history remains obscure.[60]

Some called the Lees "kings" of the swamp, but the Swamp King remembered today is Obediah Barber, who will be introduced further on. Both he and Lydia Stone, "Queen of the Okefenokee," were colorful characters whose reputations spread throughout the region. Miss Lydie's homestead was located on Cowhouse Island (also called Big Cowhouse Island to distinguish it from Little Cowhouse, or Chesser Island), a ten-by-three-mile area of raised land found along the north rim. Well suited for farming and cattle ranching (cowhouse is a term for "high ground"), Cowhouse was inhabited from the mid-nineteenth century by Swampers named Crews, Hickox and Thrift. The monikers Queen of Cowhouse and Queen of the Okefenokee were given to Lydia Stone, about whom we know quite a bit, in part due to town records and in part due to her very public and very memorable persona. Have her large physical size, raw strength and sometimes unladylike brutality been exaggerated here and there? Perhaps—but probably not to a large extent. Lydia Stone's life reads like a legend because that is how she lived it.

A good place to dive into all things Lydia is the hamlet of Schlatterville, east of Waycross and not far south of Cowhouse Island. There, Lydia is buried in the High Bluff Primitive Baptist Church Cemetery. Her marker in a family plot is the dominant marker in the cemetery. The tombstones in the plot face the old (and still active) church and are arranged like pieces on a chessboard, with the Queen alone taking center stage. Lydia's is the

Lydia Stone's tombstone at High Bluffs Primitive Baptist Church. *Larry Woodward, USFWS.*

tallest monument and is set back a bit from the two that flank it, in a way, ironically, foregrounding her memory. Behind these three stones are two more. Familiarity with the Queen's life explains the symbolic meaning of this positioning. One of her sisters, Nancy N. Smith, is buried to one side of her, and her first husband, D.G. "Gordon" Stone, is on the other. Behind her sister is Lydia's second husband, John Melton Crews, and beside him—behind Lydia—is the second of Crews's three wives, "Kizzie" Crews. The layout gives Lydia's second husband a back seat to her sister and Kizzie a back seat to Lydia, who occupies—rightfully so—the driver's seat.

Born in 1864, Lydia packed a lot of living into her seventy-four years. Her parents were farmers on Cowhouse Island, and she had six sisters, all of whom were large and strong—her sister Sarah was called the "ox woman." Lydia was from a very modest background but was determined not to remain that way, and this determination led her to become a millionaire.

She did this largely by purchasing timberland, first a few hundred acres on Cowhouse Island, where she set up a large farm and, later, much larger timber plots near Race Pond, a community north of Folkston, where she died in a very comfortable home.

As Lois and Richard Mays describe her, Lydia was uneducated but had good business sense, enough to know that landownership led to wealth. She collected two husbands in her lifetime, but her focus was on amassing land. She carried around both bullwhip and pistol and could be threatening to her workers, at times even denying them pay. She was not friendly to her neighbors, and when it suited her, she encroached on Hebard land in the Okefenokee. She sent her first husband, Gordon Stone, to live at the house at Race Pond while she stayed on Cowhouse Island and managed her affairs there, adding to her wealth by farming and raising cattle. Her sawmill produced lumber boards and railroad crossties, and she was in the turpentine business.

Gordon, smaller and weaker than his wife, died in 1926. Two years later, Lydia married John Melton Crews. The bride was sixty-three years old, and the groom, nicknamed "Baby Doll," was twenty-one. Just as Gordon Stone had worked for his wife, so did Baby Doll. Although he was her business partner, the Queen pulled all the strings. She had a way with words and numbers; she was quoted in the *Atlanta Journal* as proclaiming, "I never went to school but six days in my life and the pity of it is, I didn't learn anything those six days. But the man isn't living that can outfigger me."[61] She trusted cash only and she was able to salvage that cash when the market crashed in 1929.

"Miss Lydie" was not a stranger in local courthouses, where she appeared to counter several suits against her, some brought by employees. She was charged with moonshining along with her first husband, and Daniel Hebard took her to court more than once concerning land disputes. The most memorable of her legal challenges came, however, when Baby Doll was charged with manslaughter after the death of an employee. When he was convicted and sentenced to begin a fifteen- to twenty-year sentence, Lydia wasn't taking it. After serving only two and a half years, Crews was pardoned—the Queen had reportedly bribed the governor. Late in life, though, when she was practically on her death bed, Lydia transformed from a brash, pipe-smoking, land-grabbing, Baby Doll–loving Swamper into a stern by-the-book Methodist. Upon her death, Crews inherited her twenty thousand acres and hundreds of head of cattle. The Queen, who was childless, passed away nine months after an executive order founded the National Wildlife Refuge and a decade before the Okefenokee Swamp Park was opened on Cowhouse Island—her life was long enough to see many changes in the Okefenokee rim, indeed.

Henry Obediah Barber, called "Obediah" or "Obe," was the King of the Okefenokee. A son of the Primitive Baptist elder Isaac Barber, Obediah (sometimes spelled "Obadiah") was born in 1825 and died in 1909. Such a long life, encompassing much of the nineteenth century and spilling into the twentieth, allowed Barber, who lived first on the eastern edge of the swamp and then later on the northwestern edge, to witness a century of industrial changes. Trowell has summarized this expanse of time in relation to Obediah's life:

> *Obediah Barber witnessed the economic and social changes that gradually transformed the Okefenokee frontier into a railroad society and brought industry and commercial agriculture to the Okefenokee rim. He saw the character of the endless longleaf pine-wiregrass forests change as the demand for naval stores* [a term referring to the liquid products of pine trees] *and yellow pine timber swept the great pines away. He heard stories in the 1890s of the logging of trees in the dense cypress bays in the Okefenokee Swamp by the Suwanee Canal Company, but he died just prior to the massive railroad logging operations of the Hebard Cypress Company.*[62]

Despite these manifold changes, the Barber family, like the Chessers and Lees, lived off the land by farming, hunting and raising cattle. Like them, Barber only very occasionally went into town to purchase gunpowder, salt and cloth. Unlike these other Swamper families, though, he profited from his large property and sold large quantities of farm products and farm animals, allowing him to become, as time went on, a veritable country squire.

Certain Swamper men (including "Big Math" Matthew H. Cox) are remembered for being larger and more powerful than the average person; this continued the myth of unusually tall Native people living in the swamp and was also linked to claims that the environment and lifestyle of the Okefenokee promoted excellent health and longevity. Both "Obe" and Miss Lydia were tall and powerfully built, both ran farms and both ended up wealthy. Obe is remembered, like Lydia, for his size and strength, and anecdotes about him relate to that strength as well as his fearlessness. Whereas Lydia excelled as a businessperson, Obe excelled at ranching and hunting, storytelling and serving as a guide for others into the swamp. They were larger-than-life characters and true Swampers at heart; both had personalities that were outsized and wild, like that of the Okefenokee.

Barber was married three times, fathered twenty children with two of his wives and was a justice of the peace (as his father had been), indicating that he had attained a certain level of education. By the end of his life, he owned approximately 1,500 acres around his homestead on the northwest side of the Okefenokee, where he planted corn, sugarcane, rice and sweet potatoes and raised cattle and even sheep. Like Lydia, he married a much younger person in his last marriage. Unlike with Lydia, this spouse divorced Barber after he became a "lunatic" and was sent to an invalid home in Milledgeville, Georgia. Before too long, one of his sons brought Obediah back to live with him in Ruskin, and the King subsequently died in Waycross.

Obediah was an Okefenokee guide for surveys into the swamp, including the 1857 Richard Hunter expedition, the 1875 Haines-Pendleton expedition and Henry Jackson's 1890 survey. During the Civil War, he fought with Mercer's Partisans Rangers in the Twenty-Fourth Battalion of the Georgia Cavalry. A vast storehouse of knowledge about the swamp, its flora and fauna, the King was also recognized as a fiddler and yarn-spinner. His 1870 homestead is considered the oldest Swamper home still standing and is cited as a model of that architectural style. It was occupied until 1971; in 1995, it was added to the National Register of Historic Places. Obediah is buried at Kettle Creek Cemetery in Waycross under, not surprisingly, a large headstone.

It should be obvious that Obediah Barber incarnated all the significant facets of what it meant to be a Swamper back in the day. And it is fitting to end this presentation of him with a few words about the tall tales he told and those that were told about him. Yarn-spinning was a talent ranked very highly in Swamper culture, and one of the most oft-repeated categories of tales of the swamp involved the killing of an alligator or a bear. Logically, then, the most popular tale about Obediah is about a bear. Like bears in other stories, this animal threatened Obediah's hogs—a very real concern for Swampers—and then threatened the King himself. Part of what makes this an ideal Swamper story is that his weapon was not a rifle but a lightwood knot from a pine tree. "Lightwood" or "light'ood" is the "meat" of the wood of (especially longleaf) pine trees and is known for its hardness. Using this, Barber succeeded in beating back the bear and scaring it off. Lone Thrift recounted to Francis Harper what his father had told him concerning Barber, "Ol' man Obadiah Barber was a terrible man. He could of [*sic*] told you some powerful yarns. Uncle Barber was inclined to stretch a little, make it a little worse than it was."[63] Harper must have been disappointed that Barber died not long before his arrival at the Okefenokee.[64]

7

REFUGE

In American culture, wilderness represents complete freedom—from society, rules and regulations, city life and myriad other "ills." We have seen that this freedom is a double-edged sword, since wildernesses, including swamps, also represent loneliness and danger, even death. Moreover, those seeking isolation from the noise, crowds and violence of urban areas may be joined in the wilderness, ironically, by violent persons fleeing the justice system. And the two groups—those seeking peace and those guilty of violence—may end up living in fear of each other instead of in fear of the outside world. Wilderness areas such as the Okefenokee function as crucibles for the intermingling of these two sides of human life, although much more in fiction than historical fact. What the two sides have in common, though, is the profound belief that wilderness is synonymous with freedom, escape and refuge, however tenuous.

As already noted, Muscogee Natives, at one point, had villages in the Okefenokee. For at least several decades in the mid- to late nineteenth century, stories were told of Seminoles who escaped to the swamp to flee trouble or run away after contributing to it. Natives were not the only group, however, to find—whether in fact or fiction—refuge in the swampland. Confederate draft evaders, deserters, outlaws and escaped prisoners led to the belief that the swamp was a haven for undesirables and deviants of all sorts.

It is known that runaway enslaved people from north of the Okefenokee passed through the swamp on their way to freedom in Florida. But while historians and archaeologists know the Great Dismal Swamp in North

Carolina and Virginia served as a temporary refuge for enslaved people, we do not have concrete evidence that this was the case in the Okefenokee. This is most likely partly due to the fact that the white settlers who lived near the swamp before the Civil War were mostly poor and did not own enslaved persons. There were, however, "refugee" plantation owners from coastal Georgia who moved to the swamp rim during the Civil War, and they probably had enslaved people with them. These cases were not numerous, though, and—again—there is no clear evidence that any of them escaped into the swamp for any period.

An example of a story that did circulate and that probably has some factual basis is that of a person who was enslaved by a Johns family and who was stolen and spent some time on an island on the eastern side of the swamp. McQueen and Mizell wrote:

> *Another interior island is "John's Negro Island," and gets its name from the fact that a negro was stolen from J.J. Johns of Charlton county, during times of slavery and carried to this island and kept for several days by the thief, who intended later to carry him off and sell him. The negro and the man who stole him were finally tracked into the Swamp and discovered on this island.*[65]

Related to this, among Francis Harper's papers at Georgia Southern University is a copy of a map that was drawn by Geoffrey W. Crickmay for the Georgia Geological Survey in 1937. Someone, presumably Harper, has written on it, "John [N-word] Is."[66]

In terms of criminals, Lois B. Mays relates that W.T. Chesser sought refuge from a manslaughter charge in the swamp in 1858. According to her, the case had been dropped without him being aware.[67] Moreover, in his memoir, John Hopkins, who hired convict labor at times for Hebard, wrote, "Escaped convicts seemed to feel that Okefenokee was a good place to earn a livelihood while being well hidden."[68] He adds that he turned in some of these men. Near the swamp, the large Baxter and Company sawmill founded at Fargo in 1900 had more than one thousand convict workers who were leased from the state as part of the convict lease system. This system functioned in some southern states until the 1930s and mostly farmed out Black convicts to working camps in railroad and lumber mill companies. Georgia outlawed the practice in 1908, replacing it with the roadside chain gang system. It is said that at least one convict escaped from the Fargo camp in 1903, and it is possible that there were more. Stories are found here and there in local newspapers of both Black and white outlaws who fled into the Okefenokee before being apprehended or who escaped into it after breaking out of jail. But gangs of white outlaws, also called marauders or bandits in the 1830s and 1840s, seem to have mostly stayed on the rim of the swamp, barely penetrating it.

At the time of the Civil War, a number of men who lived near the Okefenokee as well as other parts of the South determined that the North-South conflict was not a cause worth dying for—or that their families would not be able to survive without them present or at least able to return on occasion. In Georgia, these draft dodgers and deserters often fled into the swamps or hills and mountains of their local areas. There is evidence that during the 1860s, a number of draft evaders and deserters lived for short periods in the Okefenokee. The *New Georgia Encyclopedia* informs readers, "The southern part of the state was [also] periodically plagued with guerrilla violence, and the swamps and pine barrens of South Georgia provided hiding places for deserters, draft evaders, and Unionists. The Okefenokee Swamp was another refuge for individuals and small groups of men, although the number of draft evaders or deserters who hid there is impossible to determine."[69] Furthermore, historian David Carlson has written that "deserter countries," or remote areas exploited as havens for draft evaders, existed throughout the South. These deserters sometimes poached livestock from farmers on the swamp's rim; at other times, they were aided and abetted by local inhabitants. Others were even able to remain in contact with their families who lived on the swamp's rim.

An example of a search for deserters occurred when Major George Washington Lee and his Mounted Rangers spent four months between 1864 and 1865 in South Georgia. They captured several men on Blackjack Island in the Okefenokee: "Living in fortified encampments, some still standing almost two decades later, they survived off deer, fish, alligator, and wildcat, as well as cattle stolen from farms on the edges of the swamp."[70] In the same way that runaway enslaved people were apprehended by slave patrols with "negro dogs," military deserters were chased down by dogs. There was a fear that deserters and what enslaved people there were in the area might form alliances. It was true, Carson has noted, that white evaders sometimes formed bands and gangs that robbed stores and spread terror.

Charles Pendleton described the Okefenokee guide Ben Yarborough, discussed in part III, as a deserter who lived in the swamp in an 1888 article in the *Atlanta Constitution*:

When summoned to the front in '61 he soon became disgusted at the [more] *civilized method of human butchery, and he shrank from it and sought the more congenial jungles of the* Okefeenokee [sic]. *There he became the leader of a squad of deserters and was for three years monarch of the several islands which lay deep in that dark and dismal swamp. He and his party fared well on venison, wild turkey, fish, honey, etc., which abounded thereabouts.*[71]

In 1931, Francis Harper wrote of Confederate deserters in the Okefenokee who belonged to the Chesser family:

Mrs. Allen Chesser said that three of Granddaddy (W.T.) Chesser's sons— Buck, Bill, and Tom—were in the Confederate Army, but left and came back here. They stayed out in the swamp—probably out in the "prairie houses"—and rations were "toted" to them. Before they came back from the army, they threw their guns into the river. When they arrived home, they were barefooted and nearly naked. Family members would watch the slough [toward the mainland] *to see if anybody was coming after the three Chesser boys.*[72]

Harper later added, "Tom Chesser described how homefolk would signal to those in hiding. The deserters would deposit deer or other game where their relatives could get it and leave, say, grits in exchange. Neither party saw the other. Tom said deserters stayed 'all about the swamp,' particularly in the area northwest and west of the island."[73] It is not especially surprising that members of Swamper families sought refuge from the Civil War, since they were poor and could not have enslaved people if they wanted to. In addition, they had come to live in the swamp precisely to avoid larger society and its interference in people's lives.

We have seen how the Okefenokee was envisioned and used by individuals as a refuge from society and its legal system. The term *refuge* may indicate, as well, an area of wilderness set aside so that humans may not harm it; this is the sense of the word in the name Okefenokee National Wildlife Refuge. ONWR, created in 1937, is a refuge *from* humans, not *for* them. How the National Wildlife Refuge came to be is a fascinating story that spans more than one decade and involves federal, state and local government entities; conservation groups; a Black Civilian Conservation Corps company; and many other groups and individuals who believed that the Okefenokee was worth preserving. The rise of environmentalism in the late nineteenth and early twentieth centuries did not mean, however, that the desire to use the swamp for commercial or other "progress" simply disappeared. Groups still occasionally urged that the swamp's ecosystem should be disrupted so the area could, at the least, be easily traversed. These parallel developments—the will to protect the Okefenokee and the will to subdue it—did not end, even with the opening of ONWR. And if we consider the type of disruption to the Okefenokee rim that mining companies envisioned in the 1990s and now envision the 2020s, it is clear that this controversy continues today.

During the same years that men like Jackson and Hebard saw natural lands in terms of commercial profit, an opposite vision of wilderness areas began to take hold. Yellowstone had been established as the first National Park in 1872, and the first National Wildlife Refuge opened under President Theodore Roosevelt in 1903 on Pelican Island, a small island in Florida. The National Park Service, dating from Woodrow Wilson's administration, was reorganized under the presidency of Teddy Roosevelt's cousin Franklin Delano Roosevelt. This Roosevelt also oversaw the enactment of a slew of other conservation acts. As for nongovernment conservation organizations, the Audubon Society was formed in 1886 (renamed the National Audubon Society in 1905), and the Sierra Club dates to 1892. From the late nineteenth century, then, the will to preserve ran on a parallel track beside the will to profit. In terms of the Okefenokee, the conservation track overtook the commercial one in the 1930s.

There are many significant stops on the road that led to the establishment of ONWR, and not all can be covered here.[74] In 1929, Georgia senator Walter J. Harris introduced a bill in the U.S. Senate to establish the Okefenokee Wildlife and Fish Refuge. The Senate sent members of the Forest Reservation Commission to the Okefenokee, and these officials recommended its purchase. The committee's report mentioned calls for the preservation of the swamp, which Francis Harper had already urged in his 1917 article "Okefinokee Swamp as a Reservation." Senator Harris died unexpectedly in office in 1932, however, and these efforts fizzled. At the same time, a bill was introduced into the U.S. House of Representatives to purchase the swamp for a National Park, but congresspersons from Georgia held up this process.

In the early 1930s, two plans for disturbing the Okefenokee ecosystem by creating routes through the swamp were proposed. One was an Atlantic–Gulf of Mexico canal through the swamp that reminds us of similar plans drawn up in the nineteenth century. Closely on the heels of this, the Georgia legislature considered a scenic highway through the Okefenokee.

A report encouraging the development of this "Okefenokee Scenic Highway" describes it as a forty-five-and-a-half-mile route connecting Waycross to Lake City, Florida, cutting right through the swamp. The main advantage cited would be an alternative route for tourism, commerce and military purposes between states north of Georgia and middle Florida. The disposable income of visitors who drove to southern Florida every year was mentioned as something to capitalize on. Why shouldn't South Georgia benefit from this? It was also asserted that the construction jobs created would take several hundred men off the Georgia Depression-era relief rolls. The project was placed on hold, however, after the Okefenokee Preservation Society, founded in 1918, and others pushed for the federal government itself to purchase the swamp.[75]

John Hopkins, still working for the Hebards, was instrumental in the decision not to fund this highway. A road would have surely helped remove logs, but the logs were gone, and Hopkins had set his sights on protecting the Okefenokee. Around the same time, the Georgia Society of Naturalists engaged the support of Daniel Hebard and his son, Frederick V, as part of its conservation efforts. Their lobbying in Washington, D.C., resulted in a suspension of the canal plan previously mentioned. Obviously, the fact that the Okefenokee had been stripped of commercially viable logs must have contributed to Hopkins's and the Hebards' eagerness to seek the protection of the swamp, but there is no reason to think that they were not sincere in wanting to preserve the Okefenokee.

Jean Harper regularly accompanied her husband to the Okefenokee and, like her husband, cared immensely for its preservation. She had been a nanny for the Roosevelt children when they lived at Hyde Park, and she used this connection to direct FDR's attention to the swamp. In a letter from November 1933, she wrote:

> *Dear Mr. Roosevelt,*
> *There is a matter that needs your immediate attention—the preservation of the Okefinokee Swamp....For twenty odd years naturalists and nature lovers have been working for the preservation of this marvellous [sic] wilderness; unique in its nature not only in this country, but in the world....Two years ago the Senate Committee on Wild Life Resources visited the Okefinokee and submitted a report...recommending its purchase as a national wild-life refuge. But because of the depression, nothing further has been done....We now learn of the project to put a ship canal through the swamp.*[76]

FDR commiserated in his reply, but it was only after she wrote again in early 1935 that he informed her that he had asked J.N. Darling to encourage Congress to act. Two years later, on March 30, 1937, Executive Order 7593 created the three-hundred-thousand-acre Okefenokee Wildlife Refuge. It was to be run by the Bureau of Sport Fisheries and Wildlife—later the U.S. Fish and Wildlife Service—under the Department of the Interior.

John Hopkins was able to note that at midnight on the last day of November 1936, the lands still held by the Hebards passed into the hands of the federal government. The Forest Service's final offer of $1.50 per acre was accepted by the family, meaning that the land was purchased for about $400,000. Hopkins reports that about thirty claims had to be settled or disproved before this final process could be completed, so it had not been an easy road. Upon its establishment, ONWR was managed by Hopkins until a regular manager could be named. When Earle R. Greene became the first official manager, Hopkins became "agent in charge."

The importance during the National Wildlife Refuge's very early years of Civilian Conservation Corps Company 1433 cannot be exaggerated. This group of 181 Black men virtually brought ONWR into being. The Civilian Conservation Corps was created in March 1933 under the Federal Security Administration, and most of the camps were discontinued in June 1942, due to the United States entering World War II. The CCC's goal was to provide a living wage to men who were unemployed due to the Great Depression. Initially, workers were assigned throughout the United States to aid the Forest Service, which sponsored most camps, in its land management and conservation efforts. This was accomplished primarily through the planting of trees, since, by the 1930s, more and more people understood the devastation left in the wake of industrial lumbering across wilderness areas. The U.S. Army oversaw organization at CCC camps, so the corps acquired the moniker the "Tree Army."

One of the sons of Edgar Jones, an FSA (Farm Security Administration) client in Woodville, Greene County, Georgia. He worked at a Civilian Conservation Corps camp in the summer of 1941. *Jack Delano, Library of Congress, Prints and Photographs Division.*

On the whole, the Civilian Conservation Corps is recognized as a very positive component of American history, in particular in terms of the nation's system of National Parks, National Wildlife Refuges and National Monuments. Two hundred thousand Black men participated nationwide in the CCC, about 10 percent of the organization's total membership. Almost all CCC camps were segregated, especially in the South, but the very fact that Black CCC units existed identifies the corps as being a step ahead on a long and ongoing struggle toward racial equality. For those who understand the significance of the Okefenokee Swamp as a wetland and the importance of federally designated protected areas, remembering the men of Company 1433 is essential.

There were five CCC camps around the edge of the swamp. Four of these had white recruits and were located at Fargo, Homeland, Toledo and St. George. A camp at Litard Bridge in the Osceola National Forest (near Taylor, Florida) was a Black company, as was the Folkston ("Okefenokee") company that worked at ONWR. A smaller white company located on the west side of the Swamp near Fargo, Camp BS-1Company 1448, also had a positive impact on the National Wildlife Refuge. One of this company's main jobs was to improve the road from Fargo to Jones Island, where the Stephen C. Foster State Park was established in 1954. The Fargo company also built towers and firebreaks and fought fires.

Camp Okefenokee, formed of 181 men, was transferred from a camp in Douglas, Georgia, and waited for the construction of a minimal camp on the site of Henry Jackson's Camp Cornelia. It was soon determined, however, that the structures were not up to par. Camp Okefenokee was then built by and for Company 1433. The site chosen was four to five miles east of Camp Cornelia, along the Folkston Highway (also now called the Okefenokee Parkway).

In addition to Camp Okefenokee, Company 1433 constructed a site at the old Camp Cornelia where administrators and staff worked and lived and where the public had convenient nearby access to boating and other activities. A few of these structures remain today. Life at Camp Okefenokee followed the same routine as it did at other CCC camps across the nation. Saturdays were spent cleaning up the camp; Sundays were the men's one day off a week. On weekday evenings, enrollees took classes in math, typing, reading and other subjects. Every six months, they earned six days of leave, which most used to return home to their families. The work in the Okefenokee accomplished on weekdays included the demolishing of the remaining buildings at Camp Cornelia and the construction there of administration and services buildings, cabins, latrines, furniture and other

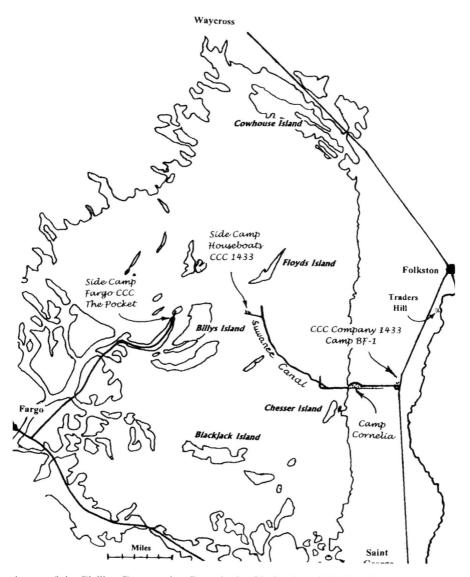

A map of the Civilian Conservation Corps in the Okefenokee. *Chris Trowell.*

structures for use by ONWR. John Hopkins noted in one of his quarterly reports for the refuge in 1941 that "only dead and down" cypress was used for this construction. The 1927 log cabin at Camp Cornelia occupied by Hopkins when Hebard had sawmills there was modernized by the CCC.

The first administration building of ONWR, constructed by Camp Okefenokee of the Civilian Conservation Corps. *Larry Woodward, USFWS.*

In 1983, it was placed in the National Register of Historic Places. The application for the National Register of Historic Places noted that this cabin is the "last remaining tangible evidence left in the area of the man most closely associated with the initial periods of exploration, exploitation, and eventual preservation of the Okefenokee Swamp."

A dock, boathouse and parking lot at Camp Cornelia were also constructed by Company 1433. Trees were planted and transplanted and area fences and cattle guards installed, partly because National Refuges were required to have visible boundaries and partly to keep wild hogs from attacking the cattle that grazed on the other side (the private side) of the boundary. CCC workers put in telephone and power lines and built chicken houses and firebreaks. New water wells were drilled, roads were constructed just outside the boundaries of the National Wildlife Refuge and picnic shelters erected at Camp Cornelia and Coffee Bay. Working along the Jackson's Folly canal, many of the workers spent five days a week hauling up what had been abandoned in the canal over the previous decades, including large machinery, logs and brush and trees that had grown up or fallen down over the years. They also worked at expanding a water trail—although not the full canal—farther west so that boats could reach Billy's Lake, the largest

The John Hopkins Cabin, Camp Cornelia. *Larry Woodward, USFWS.*

open-water lake in the swamp. As part of this, workers removed a low dam that had been constructed by the Suwanee Canal Company at the end of the west fork of the canal. The workers assigned to this had a side camp on the canal, so they did not have to commute back and forth to Camp Okefenokee. Barges were converted into houseboats for them, and they returned to the main residential camp on the weekends.[77]

We are fortunate that as part of his interviews with CCC workers, an employee of the U.S. Fish and Wildlife Service named Dennis Holland transcribed a telephone interview that he did with one of the men assigned to Camp Okefenokee. Henry Taylor of Elko, Georgia, spent September 1939–September 1941 at the National Wildlife Refuge. He was interviewed in 1999 at the age of seventy-nine. The interview provides a wealth of information about daily life, work and conditions at the camp.[78] Taylor did not work with the canal crew but was able to provide information on their activities and other projects. He could usually be found at Camp Okefenokee, where he was a blacksmith. After leaving the CCC, Taylor worked as an auto mechanic in the Army and Air Force and then continued as a mechanic for the United States Postal Service in Michigan. He returned to Georgia after retiring from the Postal Service.

Civilian Conservation Corps workers earned thirty dollars a month, twenty-five of which they sent home. Henry Taylor mentioned that of the five dollars they kept, he saved three per month, as did other workers. He asserted in the interview that he enjoyed and gained much from his stint with the CCC: "loved it"; "[but] we enjoyed it. I enjoyed every moment of it"; "my whole life in the CCC was a wonderful thing." Race did not come up in the interview, but we may infer that it had something to do with the workers being banned from Trader's Hill, where they had gone for entertainment and relaxation in the early part of Taylor's time in the company. Trader's Hill became "off limits" after a fellow "tree trooper"—a term for CCC workers—was shot in the shoulder by someone in the village. Subsequently, the men were allowed to spend one weekend a month in either Jacksonville or Waycross. The praise of these men by National Refuge officials and the local newspaper was extremely positive, despite whatever may have happened at Trader's Hill.

Camp Okefenokee operated until the end of October 1941. In 1942, John Hopkins wrote in a quarterly report for the National Wildlife Refuge, "Development work for the Refuge will probably be negligible for the 'duration' [of World War II]." When Pearl Harbor was attacked in December 1941, the CCC camp had already been disbanded. Taylor was in basic training with the Army and noted in the interview how well the CCC had prepared him for communal life in the Army. There remains much to be investigated and publicized about the men of Company 1433 and their lives in the Okefenokee. Fortunately, in October 2023, it was announced that the federal government, due to the perseverance of Georgia senator Raphael Warnock, provided almost $500,000 to fund research into this camp of the CCC and to raise public awareness of this long-neglected part of Georgia history.

ONWR has had an important and positive economic impact on the areas surrounding the Okefenokee and, therefore, on Swamper families. Employees at the National Refuge included men from Swamper families, such as Sam Mizell, a patrolman-agent, and Bryant Crews, a patrol officer. Guy Brantly and Tommy Roddenberry were also early patrolmen. These men were significant in ending the poaching of alligators, bears and other animals, which occurred during the first decades of the National Wildlife Refuge. They also probably made the transition of most of the swamp from privately held land to public lands smoother than it may have been otherwise.

In the 1960s, the Suwannee Canal Recreational Area replaced Camp Cornelia as the designation for the National Wildlife Refuge's public services, including a visitors' center and private concession. A new ONWR headquarters, no longer within Camp Cornelia per se, was built in 1978, and then a newer one in 1996. In 1972, the Wilderness Canoe Trail System of the National Wildlife Refuge was developed, allowing visitors a chance to get to know the Okefenokee in depth. There are, at present, over one hundred miles of canoe trails in ONWR and ten overnight camping platforms. In 1974, the Okefenokee National Wilderness Area was established; its boundaries are a bit different than those of the National Wildlife Refuge, and it extends more protections than ONWR can. In 1990, the Okefenokee Wildlife League (OWL) formed as an advocate nonprofit group for the National Wildlife Refuge that now operates as the Friends of the Okefenokee Wildlife Refuge. Finally, another important area group that has formed is the Greater Okefenokee Association of Landowners (GOAL), organized in 1994. This is a grassroots organization that promotes stewardship of the land within and around the swamp.

Plans for mining titanium dioxide on the edge of the Okefenokee—by the Dupont Corporation in the 1990s and Twin Pines Minerals of Alabama today—have twice put fear into the hearts of people for whom the conservation of the Okefenokee Swamp is of the highest importance. Although the proposed area is outside the National Wildlife Refuge and Wilderness Area, it is situated on the south part of Trail Ridge. Incursion into the ridge poses a potentially serious threat to the species that depend on the hydrology of the swamp.

The Okefenokee National Wildlife Refuge entrance sign. *Jeffrey Isaac Greenberg/Alamy stock photograph.*

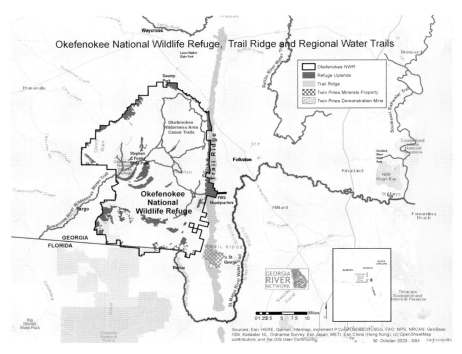

A map showing the Okefenokee National Wildlife Refuge, Trail Ridge and the proposed Twin Pines LLC mining site. *Georgia River Network.*

In 2022, Debra Haaland—the first U.S. secretary of the Department of the Interior of Native origin—wrote to the governor of Georgia, Brian Kemp, to express her opposition to this mining project. In this way, she followed in the footsteps of Secretary of the Interior Bruce Babbitt, who voiced his opposition to the projected DuPont mine back in 1997. Babbitt had visited ONWR, as has Haaland, who expressed her concerns not only about the ecosystem and hydrology of the Okefenokee but also about its historical and cultural significance: "The swamp is also part of the Muscogee (Creek) Nation ancestral homeland and is recognized as a significant and important Traditional Cultural Property. Current tribal members recognize that the Trail Ridge landscape feature, which is included within the proposed mining boundary, was likely used as a travel corridor by their ancestors." In addition, she stated, burial grounds located on the ridge deserve protection.[79]

The accidental drainage and other problems likely to be associated with any mining done in the Okefenokee area, especially on or near Trail Ridge, could very well make Jackson's Folly look benign.

PART III

CULTURE

8

SPEECH, WORSHIP, SONG

Part III investigates two forms of culture in and around the Okefenokee. First, you will read about the cultural practices of those who live in the swamp and its uplands. Sometimes, these practices are shared with larger southern communities; at other times, they seem especially characteristic of swamplands or even the Okefenokee exclusively. Manifestations of Swamper culture include the use of particular language and speech patterns, folklore and tall tales and musical and religious traditions. The last chapter is about cultural expressions, mostly books and movies, that are set in the Okefenokee. These have been produced by outsiders as well as local residents. The 1941 film *Swamp Water* is a result of the efforts of both of these populations: it is based on a novel penned by a local, but the film had a French director and was produced by a Hollywood studio.

Okefenokee Swampers developed unique terms and expressions, some that have died out over the years, some that have not. Cultures worldwide that are isolated from urban and cosmopolitan influences retain archaic language features longer than "city folk" do. The inhabitants also develop novel uses of both vocabulary and sentence structure. Some Okefenokee rim examples are shared by regional communities, such as the "cracker" culture of southern Georgia and northern Florida, Appalachia or the South in general. During his visits in the early twentieth century, biologist Francis Harper became fascinated with not only the plants and animals of the swamp but also Swamper folklore, including its colorful use of words. We are fortunate that Delma Presley compiled a glossary of Swamper terms found in Harper's notebooks, and most of the following examples come from *Okefinokee Album*.[80]

Many of the distinctive terms that the Chessers, Lees, Mizells and Thrifts employed—and in some cases still do—were related to their natural surroundings. These families lived immersed in nature, obtaining their sustenance from and learning to adapt to the particular environment of the land of the trembling earth. Swampers gave birds colorful names: *shakybag* (Carolina wren), *swamp canary* (prothonotary warbler), *butter-ball* (ring-necked duck) and *good-God* or *Kate* (pileated woodpecker). For obvious reasons, *swamp* was added to various animal names: *swamp thrasher* (brown thrasher), *swamp rabbit* (marsh rabbit) and *swamp rat* (rice rat). Some terms echo the language of the English, Scottish, Welsh and/or Irish ancestors of the Swampers, including *afyeard* (afraid), *chivaree* (serenade), *hobbiedehoy* (irresponsible youth), *trumpery* (utensils and bedding) and *progue* (to explore).

More typically southern terms include *disremember* (forget), *fixing to* (ready to), *pinder* (peanut), *light'ood* (lightwood, fatwood or pine knot of a dead pine tree), *painter* (panther), *prairie* (wet grassland), *haint* or *booger* (ghost) and *sham-shack* (red-bellied woodpecker). *Catheads* (biscuits) is typically Appalachian. Words could also identify a specific Swamper family. Harper notes, for example, that the Chessers called the great blue heron a *preacher*, while on Billys Island the bird was called a *po'jo* or *po'job*.

Language and the telling of tales are intricately related, and this is evident in Swamper storytelling. The simplicity of the legends, tales and yarn-spinning of the Okefenokee belies their importance for building and maintaining community. The gift of gab, combined with the talent of persuasion required of Okefenokee storytellers, is, at its core, a cracker practice. The English and Scottish origin of this term dates to William Shakespeare's time: *Crackers* were people who talked and talked, evidently for the pure pleasure of putting words together. In the United States, "The Scotch-Irish who settled the southern frontier were called 'Crackers' by the British authorities."[81] The term refers to white rural residents—usually farmers and ranchers—who lead mostly self-sufficient lives tied to the land. They adhered to traditions practiced by their ancestors, passed down from generation to generation and shared by the community. Although *Cracker* has been used pejoratively as a racial slur to stigmatize poor, rural whites, it also retains a positive flavor for many Swampers.

A good deal of the most popular Okefenokee yarns highlight the prowess of men and hunting dogs during encounters with alligators, bears or wildcats. Told about family members and locals, they present interactions with dangerous animals or skills at hunting or fishing in exaggerated, satirical or generally humorous ways. While there have been female raconteurs, notably Rhoda Mizell Barber, and while women and girls were certainly not excluded from audiences, this form of passing the time was generally a male activity.

The Swamper storyteller has two main goals in mind: to entertain and to outdo other storytellers in a sort of upmanship. Some of the most admired of these storytellers were Lemuel "Lem" Griffis, who wrote a tall tales series for the Clinch County newspaper; Robert Allen Chesser; and Will Cox. Griffis was so influential that some storytellers told tales about him telling stories, thus impressing listeners with the tale itself as well as their own ability to imitate the master raconteur. One Griffis yarn tells of an elderly Swamper's wooden cane, which, once bitten by a venomous snake, became so swollen that it provided crossties for ten miles of railroad:

> *We have some of the most deadly poison snakes here most any place in the world, I reckon. Uncle Paul, he come down to see us one time, and he walked with a walking cane. He went to carry one after he was ninety-six, and he was walking around through the woods out here, one of them poisonous snakes struck at his leg and hit that walking cane. He walked little ways further, noticed that walking cane to get—begin to get—heavy, and he looked at it and it was all swollen up. He couldn't carry but a little ways further, before it got so big and heavy he just had to leave it. He thought lots of his walking cane, so next morning he went down to see about it. By that time it was swollen up till it was just an enormous size log. He notified feller to have a sawmill to come get that log and saw it up into lumber. But by that time it couldn't be moved, but he moved his sawmill to it, and he sawed enough crossties outa that swollen up walking cane to build ten miles of railroad, and after he got his railroad built there come up a awful heavy rain, washed all the poison outa them crossties, and he gathered 'em up and sold 'em for toothpicks.*[82]

This story has it all: a dose of realism, humor, suspense, exaggeration, a quirky use of language and the recognition of Swamper resourcefulness.

Robert Allen Chesser's story of a "sight" of alligators is an example of a tale involving more than one animal. This tale's purpose is to astonish, and as is often the case, Chesser signaled early on that it is true, even if it seems unbelievable. In fact, this story is based on a natural event in the Okefenokee, although the number of animals is exaggerated. A sight or sighting occurs when many fish gather on the water's edge, drawing shorebirds who wait patiently for alligators, who arrive next. In this story, three hundred alligators showed up, Chesser stated, and created a "frenzy," a term used for the racket and vigorous splashing produced by a group of gators. As the fish were stirred up, first the gators and then the hundreds of birds took advantage to dine on them. Not long after, Chesser and his hunting buddies also took advantage, shooting over a dozen alligators. "And when they took a notion to get away, there was a sight to look at— when they commenced smelling the blood. They started down that road. They was that thick. I could-a-walked down that road on 'gator heads. My brother up yonder'll identify to it. It's true."[83]

Ben Yarborough, who lived in the swamp beginning in the 1830s, according to Charles Pendleton, was pronounced the most talented teller of "camp stories" in Pendleton's *Atlanta Constitution* reports of the 1875 Haines-Pendleton expedition into the Okefenokee.[84] "Uncle Ben" was chosen as guide on this trip because he "probably knows more of the swamp than any man living. He has been the guide of every exploring party and, is employed by the Constitution's expedition in the same capacity." The article continues, stating Yarborough participated in the men's storytelling in the evenings on Billys Island, outperforming the others. In another article in the Atlanta newspaper in 1888, Pendleton wrote a vivid account of Yarborough and his four dogs fighting a panther in the swamp.[85] Pendleton also called Obediah Barber "one of Uncle Ben's conferees and chums," suggesting a friendship between the tellers of tall tales. He also refers to Yarborough as "the old Negro guide," although Harper and his informants, mentioned later, do not identify Uncle Ben as a Black man.[86]

According to Hamp, Ben Yarborough, in addition to being a guide and yarn-spinner, was a "conjure doctor" who healed people and predicted the future.[87] Delma Presley tells us that Hamp met Uncle Ben when the latter was in his mid-eighties through the Primitive Baptist Church. He quoted Hamp: "When old Ben was eighty-five, he could dance and sing songs just as lively as his sons."[88] One of his treatments was to "send a telegram" to an ill person by pointing in their direction and then touching a vein in his arm. He performed cures, one for Aunt Rhodie (Rhoda Mizell Spaulding, Hamp's sister) for no charge. Hamp also stated, "A lot er the boys workin' on that Suwanee Canal would give 'im a dollar. He'd tell your fortune, or what girl yer wuz goin' to marry."[89]

Luther Thrift recounted a tale concerning Lydia Stone that his maternal grandfather had heard from Bill Joyce, a physically imposing Black man who worked for the Queen of the Okefenokee. This yarn says Bill was cutting crossties on Cowhouse Island when he decided that it was too wet for his mules to haul the crossties from the water into a wagon. Miss Lydie firmly insisted that the two of them, instead of the mules, would have to do the work. While telling the story, Bill expressed astonishment at Miss Lydie's strength.[90] In addition, in her article, folklorist Kay L. Cothran mentions a Black spinner of yarns by the name of Kato Lambert. Lambert worked in the turpentine camps of Toledo, Georgia. He told Cothran that racist tales of some white Swampers featured disturbing physical "humor" involving Black men's corpses and/or lynchings. Black men have unfortunately been remembered less for their gift of yarn-spinning and more for the presence of their maimed bodies in some Swamper tales.[91]

Many Swampers were Primitive Baptists, and the latter church's distinct traditions have left especially strong marks on Okefenokee culture. Swamper families belonged (and many still belong) to the Crawfordite tradition of the Primitive Baptist Church, the more conservative branch. Okefenokee rim Primitive Baptists practice foot washing and a cappella four-note singing. In their churches, which are constructed of wood, parishioners sit on wooden benches surrounded by unadorned walls. In his book on the history of wiregrass Primitive Baptists, John Crowley wrote of Crawfordites, "Their meetinghouses are still unlighted, unceiled, unpainted, and completely unheated."[92]

Traditional Primitive Baptists have a unique way of singing, practiced during church services and during "sings" at their meetinghouses and homes. This is called, variously, Sacred Harp, shape-note, four-note or lined-hymn singing. The notation system is a simplified form that uses only four notes, represented on the page by simple geometric shapes. This singing was imported to the South from New England and was encouraged as an accessible way for uneducated parishioners to read music. The shape notes align with four voice registers: tenor (what is normally called treble), bass, soprano (normally called tenor) and alto. A leader "pitches the notes," first calling two lines of notes and then the corresponding two lines of lyrics; church attendees repeat after each couplet. The singing is slow, has no instrumental accompaniment and may sound monotonous to the uninitiated.[93]

Before the Civil War, the few families in the area who enslaved people brought them to church services, where they were listed in the records as "the property of" so-and-so. After the war, however, the former enslaved persons' surnames were listed. At this time, Black churchgoers began to

Sardis Primitive Baptist Church, where many Swampers are buried. *Larry Woodward, USFWS.*

form their own Primitive Baptist churches. Crowley remarked that both Black and white churches, in the past and now, feature elders (all men) who spontaneously "chant their sermons....These churches and ministers believe that the chanted delivery is indicative of divine inspiration."[94]

Two of the well-known church leaders on the edge of the swamp were Elder Moses Thrift at Mount Olive Primitive Baptist Church on the west side and Elder W.O. Gibson at Sardis Primitive Baptist Church on the east side. Francis Harper referred to Gibson as "probably the most intelligent man in Charleton County."[95] His church, Sardis Church, is one of the oldest in the Okefenokee area. The congregation was formed in 1819 at Trader's Hill, and the first church building to be constructed at the present location was erected around 1840. Circuit rider preachers were not uncommon in the past, given that small communities were often dispersed over great

Harry, Kate, Roxie and Tom Chesser at a sing with the four-note book (1944). They are using the Sacred Harp book. *Francis Harper, Zach S. Henderson Library Special Collections, Georgia Southern University.*

A sing at the Chesser homestead. Bernice Rodenberry and her daughters sing from the Sacred Harp book at the annual Chesser homestead open house, 1997. *Laurie Kay Sommers, South Georgia Folklife Project Photographic Collection, Valdosta State Archives and Special Collections.*

distances. The custom was for four Primitive Baptist churches to organize together, each holding a Saturday "conference," where business matters were discussed, and a Sunday service one weekend per month. On both days, four-note singing was heard, with communion and foot washing reserved for Sunday. The monthly service did not mean that people only attended church monthly. Before automobiles, parishioners would travel to other churches in the area for the three other weekends, often spending the night in local homes. This created occasions for visiting and socializing. Once a year, an annual meeting was (and is) held, which was also a time of social and spiritual activities. The practice continues that to become a member of the church, a person must have a dream or a vision that inspires them; remaining a nonmember but attending services is not frowned upon. This comes from the fact that Primitive Baptists do not seek to convert others but rely on individuals to recognize divine inspiration.

The author of this book was fortunate enough to attend weekend services at High Bluff Primitive Baptist Church, where Lydia Stone was buried, in 2023. A business meeting, which attracted mostly members, was held on Saturday morning, while a service on Sunday morning was attended by members and many non-members. On both days, women and men members sat on opposite sides of the pulpit, while nonmembers of both genders sat in benches facing the pulpit. Women brought seat cushions, and men hung their hats on nails protruding from wooden beams. Tobacco spit holes in the floorboards on the men's side are a thing of the past at High Bluff. Small hymnals of "primitive songs" were used for a cappella line singing. Spontaneous sermons, given by two elders in a chanting style, were also characteristic of both days.

We may get a feeling for the old-time church service from what Hamp Mizell told Harper in the early 1930s about his cousin Jack: "Ol' man Jack—j'ined the church erlong erbout Wed. It uza big meetin' time—it jes' kep' in motion, yer know. It rocked on up till erbout Fri., an there uz conference the nex'day." Harper called the Lees "holy rollers" and took photographs of their baptisms in Billy's Lake. He wrote, "Eventually that very worthy fellow, Jackson Lee [of Billys Island], seemed to succumb to emotional insanity brought on by Holy-Rollerism." No insanity was noted by this author at High Bluff Primitive Baptist Church, however, whose congregants were very welcoming.[96]

The same Hamp Mizell was known as the troubadour of the Okefenokee. The word *troubadour* comes from a southern dialect of medieval French and means "(singing) poet," or "composer." Okefenokee troubadours

Inside Sardis Primitive Baptist Church. Nails for men's hats and spit holes in the floor are visible. *Larry Woodward, USFWS.*

such as Hamp Mizell played the fiddle or banjo and sang ballads. He told Francis Harper, "I reckon I've wrote out a thousand ballads for people, just to keep 'em a-goin'. If it wasn't for me—I don't want to brag—I reckon they'd a-died out."[97] Hamp was also a "set-caller" at frolics, or gatherings for square dancing that Swampers enjoyed on Friday or Saturday evenings at various homesteads. Banjo players and fiddlers provided music for songs with colorful titles, such as two listed by Luther Thrift: "Three Hands 'Round and Shoot the 'Gator" and "Peavine Swing and a Grapevine Exchange."[98] Hamp Mizell reported to Harper that a ballad named "The Billy's Island Boys" was performed by Lee boys on the island; it was a version of a classic ballad, "The Piney Woods Boys."[99]

Of Dutch origin, the word *frolic* means "to make merry." As a noun, it has become associated with dances where merrymaking is de rigueur, especially in Appalachia and the South. Unlike at church services, musical instruments such as the fiddle and banjo were welcomed at frolics. Francis Harper observed, "Old-fashioned square dances or frolics seem to have been held all through the Okefinokee region as far back as anyone can remember. They are said to have flourished particularly among the young folk of the

Opposite, top: Hamp Mizell with a fiddle on his porch, May 17, 1930. *Francis Harper papers, Kenneth Spencer Research Library, University of Kansas.*

Opposite, bottom: Women and men dancing and playing music in the yard. *Francis Harper papers, Kenneth Spencer Research Library, University of Kansas.*

Above: Hamp Mizell demonstrates his two-mile swamp holler. *Francis Harper papers, Kenneth Spencer Research Library, University of Kansas.*

'Hardshell' or Primitive Baptist communities. These dances go by the name of 'breakdown,' not "Virginia reel."'[100] At frolics, young and old, men, women and children, would gather to socialize and "gambol" (not gamble) and thus strengthen community ties. This music had an entertainment function, whereas Sacred Harp music had a spiritual one.

"Hollering" or "hollerin'," an outdoor vocalization that resembles yodeling, was practiced by some Swampers (at least the men). A traditional practice in many Appalachian and Southern communities, hollering may involve lengthy calls that serve to communicate or even entertain. David Lee was an expert at the "'Billy's Island Yell,' a signal used by visitors or those returning home to Billys Island."[101] Hamp Mizell also excelled at the practice. Specific hollers were generally used to signal the near arrival of a hunter or hunters or to alert potentially suspicious neighbors that a friend was approaching. Hearing the loud and unusual call in a place as deserted of other humans as the Okefenokee must have been both an impressive and eerie experience. As a family tradition, though, it provided reassurance and would have been heard as melodic, even beautiful.

9

SWAMP FICTIONS

The multiple and sometimes contradictory images that American culture has developed surrounding swamplands appear in novels and stories, short and feature films, painted and drawn images and photographs of places like the Okefenokee. In American culture, swamps elicit emotions ranging from tranquility and comfort to fear and even terror. When we think of swamps, we think of nature in its pristine form, innocent and beautiful, but we also see it as dark and potentially deadly. The swamp is an escape from the problems that come with living in a densely populated area, but it is also a space devoid of the support and protections afforded by society. That human habitation is difficult—sometimes impossible—in swamplands adds to the sense that there is something unnatural about these ecosystems, something monstrous and unknowable, something enticing yet highly dangerous. Whether visual or written, tales of the swamp have participated in creating an image of the Okefenokee as a landscape that generates a rich and contradictory source of ideas concerning human interactions with nature.

Swamps have been a favorite setting for fictions that appeal to an American understanding of independence and fortitude, expansion and exploration, this against the backdrop of a potentially dangerous natural world. Cultural expressions have contributed to keeping the imagined Jekyll and Hyde sides of swamps alive. Substantial stories—as distinct from tall tales—have told of transient inhabitants of the swamp seeking escape from the evils of human society as well as those whose own ignoble natures introduce a new peril to the swamp. In certain stories, swamplands provide a place of refuge; in others, they take revenge on those who dare enter.[102]

Louis Beauregard Pendleton, although rarely remembered today, was a prolific and fairly popular writer of Southern literature in the late nineteenth and early twentieth centuries. He used the Okefenokee as a setting for stories more than any other novelist; we might even call him the King of Swamp Fiction. During Pendleton's lifetime, swamp fiction belonged, for the most part, to a genre that appealed to him: the boy's adventure book. His intimate knowledge of the Okefenokee allowed him to add this place to the list of wildernesses favored by publishers of this book genre.

Born in 1861, Pendleton belonged to an important Valdosta family. His father, Philip C. Pendleton, ran a farm, was postmaster and founded the *South Georgia Times*, a weekly. His mother was Catherine Tebeau. These two families are remembered by historians of Waycross, which was first called Pendleton (where an early rail station was located) and then Tebeauville. When Philip Pendleton died, his sons Lewis Beauregard and Charles Rittenhouse renamed the news weekly the *Valdosta Times* and made it a daily. Charles then took over this paper and later ran the *Macon Telegraph*. He was the Pendleton of the 1875 Haines-Pendleton Expedition into the Okefenokee, and he penned the *Atlanta Constitution* articles on this trip, signing them C.R.P. His brother Lewis changed the spelling of his first name to "Louis" because he was a Francophile, that is, a connoisseur of all things French. He worked with Charles on the *Macon Telegraph*, penned a biography of Alexander H. Stephens (vice-president of the Confederacy), wrote novels and died in Pennsylvania, where he had moved, in 1939.

We may assume that Pendleton's Okefenokee fiction reflects some of the adventures he had with his numerous brothers in the swamp when they were young. Trowell states that Charles and Louis made a trip into the swamp in 1893 and that this, along with Charles's conversations with his brother about his participation in the 1875 expedition, influenced the fiction Louis subsequently produced.[103] Two novels set in the Okefenokee are *King Tom and the Runaways: The Story of What Befell Two Boys in a Georgia Swamp* (1890) and *In the Okefenokee: A Story of Wartime and the Great Georgia Swamp* (1898). Set around the time of the Civil War, both feature fatherless teenage boys and their adventures tracking down escapees in the swamp. In *King Tom*, the young boy "king" means to track down an enslaved man, Jim, who escaped from Tom and his widowed mother's plantation on the edge of the Okefenokee.[104] This is Tom's pretext to go into the swamp, which he had already been itching to explore. Pendleton thus draws on the romance (in the sense of literary adventure) of the runaway enslaved person as depicted in Henry Wadsworth Longfellow's poem "The Slave in the Dismal Swamp" (1842) and Harriet Beecher Stowe's *Dred: A Tale of the Great Dismal Swamp* (1856), both set in the Great Dismal Swamp, where runaway enslaved people from adjacent areas did hide.

In *In the Okefenokee*, Pendleton expanded on the boy's swamp adventure genre to include Confederate Army deserters.[105] Young teenagers Joe and Charley, the sons of a coastal refugee family, become lost in the swamp. They are captured, not by Seminoles or thieves, but by Confederate evaders who have themselves captured a runaway enslaved man in the swamp (they put him to work for them). Thus, they restage plantation life, making it clear they have not deserted the Confederate Army because they are abolitionists. Ironically, in convincing the deserters to return and fight for the honor of the South, young Joe frees the enslaved man, Asa, from them, but then returns him to his original plantation. "Sweet" Jackson, the one deserter who chooses not to return and fight for the Cause, is punished with death from a snakebite.

Born too late to have encountered actual Confederate draft evaders and runaway enslaved people in the Okefenokee, Pendleton capitalized on images of the swamp as a dark, foreboding and primitive terrain braved by humans who seek refuge from the law, whether they were enslaved or conscripted. Joe rehabilitates, we might say, both types of renegades: he shames the deserters into rejoining the fight to maintain slavery, and he convinces the enslaved to accept their low status. By shepherding both evaders and an enslaved man out of the swamp, Joe and King Tom, Pendleton's boys, repair the blurring line between nature and civilization that the escapees in the swamp had caused. Pendleton stages the swamp as a site where adolescent boys become men, first by surviving the Okefenokee's natural and man-made threats and then by returning to society men who no longer seek to defy its laws. Louis Beauregard Pendleton spent his boyhood near the Okefenokee and then demonstrated that it was a setting perfectly suited to coming-of-age stories. As Jimmy Walker and the Swampers, a local band from the 1960s and 1970s, asserted in their song "Swamp Country," the Okefenokee is a land "where a man can find his worth."

Fifty years after *King Tom*, a writer native to Cairo, Georgia, a town not far from the Okefenokee, also set an adolescent's (this time an older one's) story there in the novel *Swamp Water*. The author of short stories, Vereen Bell was also the editor of the *Youth's Companion* and *American Boy* after these two magazines merged in the 1930s. His life was cut short in 1944, when he was killed on the USS *Gambia Bay* at the Battle of Leyte Gulf in the Philippines. *Swamp Water* appeared first in installments in the *Saturday Evening Post* in late 1940 and then in book form in early 1941.

Swamp Water is the most significant novel set in the Okefenokee in terms of its poetic prose, memorable characterization and melding of setting with story. The most impressive single description of the Okefenokee in Bell's writings is found not in the novel, however, but in his short story "The Way the Swamp Looks":

> *The way the swamp looks depends on what you are doing in it. Sometimes it is beautiful. There are lovely waterways of clean black water, and great forests of green-topped cypresses, awe-filling in their straight tallness. There are wide flat prairies of bonnet-covered shallow water, where deer wade out and feed. But if you are hunting a man, the swamp is hostile and ugly, seven hundred square miles of trembling earth and bog and treacherous wasteland; with thickets so impenetrable that in them it's said you can't cock a pistol; a wild and lonely world, miles of fire-gnawed stumps and petrified logs, and bushes whose limbs grow back into the earth to form a hoop and catch a man's foot.*[106]

Bell's favorite literary subject was hunting in the swamp, and his favorite characters, in short stories and in *Swamp Water*, were hunters and their loyal dogs. In fact, *Swamp Water* begins with a young hunter, Ben Ragan, whose dog Trouble goes missing during a hunting trip; the animal disappears into the Okefenokee. This is the incident that sets the plot in motion. The contradictions of the Okefenokee—the two ways of looking at it—are experienced by Ben as he searches for the runaway Trouble and encounters trouble in the form of an escaped criminal hiding in the swamp.[107]

Bell surely knew of and was influenced by Louis B. Pendleton's work, but his writing is more literary, and he sets his fiction long past the era of war deserters and (possible) runaway enslaved people. (Although the 1941 film based on *Swamp Water* is set in the early 1940s, the novel was, according to its author, set in the 1890s.) Bell is concerned with a different kind of outlaw, a hogthief and murderer, and the young man, Ben, who proves that the murder was justified. Even after this, Tom Keefer, the outlaw, chooses to stay in the Okefenokee (unlike in the film versions), but he has been redeemed through the public acknowledgement of his innocence.

Ben goes against his father's warnings when he enters the Okefenokee to look for Trouble. His dog may be his immediate concern, but he has other long-held reasons for wanting to explore the swamp: "They said Okefenokee held danger and unspeakable terrors; and yet for Ben it was a place of weird fascination, 'I'm a-going in her,' he thought."[108] In going "into Okefenokee" and remaining in the swamp longer than his father allows, Ben also claims his independence from his father. He ends the story a man, one ready to assume a man's responsibilities. Again, the Okefenokee is an isolated and unpredictable place where boys are challenged to grow and prove themselves.

Readers eager to absorb other fiction and nonfiction set in the Okefenokee may also enjoy A.S. McQueen's *Club-Foot of the Okefenokee* (1939), although its language is less poetic and its story more farfetched than that of Bell's novel.[109] This is the tale of a young man who is hired to locate Okefenokee moonshiners and who encounters the pet bear of a beautiful Native girl. This girl, called "Swamp Angel," is not McQueen's invention or a type particular to the Okefenokee but rather a figure of legend who takes various shapes in American lore and literature. McQueen's novel seems influenced by *Freckles* (1904), one of Gene Stratton-Porter's popular novels about the Limberlost Swamp in Indiana, which has a female character with the nickname Swamp Angel. He may also have been influenced by William Bartram's account of the "Daughters of the Sun."

Contemporary writers continue to pen fictions about the Okefenokee, some by resuscitating time-worn plots, others with surprisingly novel takes on encounters between people and wildlife in the swamp. Virginia Lanier's mysteries always feature the word *bloodhound* in their titles, as a reference to the traditional character of the swamp hunting dog and to emphasize the mystery and danger of the place. Others have also penned mysteries that take place in this swamp. Children's books about the Okefenokee include the boys' adventure books already mentioned, as well as the more recent *Ladd of the Big Swamp*, by Cecile Hulse Matschat, and the "Swampy" series by Zan Heyward.

Last but not least, fictions of the Okefenokee include an unusual comic strip that entertained millions of newspaper subscribers from the late 1940s to the mid-1970s. *Pogo* began its run in the *New York Star* in 1948 and was widely syndicated in 1949. Book collections of the strip were also available beginning in 1953. The last panel of the comic appeared in newspapers in 1975. In the 1950s, college students promoted a "Pogo for President" craze, which included the formation of the Pogo Party. For many years, Pogo, the Okefenokee opossum, and his many anthropomorphized animal friends were cultural phenomena, and scores of Americans self-identified as "Pogophiles."

Walt Kelly, a cartoonist, newspaper reporter and animator for Disney, was born in Philadelphia in 1913 and grew up in Connecticut. He visited the Okefenokee Swamp Park as a special guest in 1955. The inhabitants of Kelly's swamp include Pogo Possum, a rather ordinary opossum surrounded by extraordinary characters; Howland Owl, the scientist who knows "practically everything"; Chug Curtis, the mail carrier who is also a duck; Ol' Albert, the cigar-smoking alligator and Pogo's sidekick; Porky Pine, the porcupine with a bad attitude; Cap'n Churchy la Femme, the mud turtle in a pirate hat; Beauregard Bugleboy, the officious "houn'dog"; and, finally, Miz Mam'zelle Hepzibah, the alluring French skunk who hankers after Pogo's attentions. The comic provides endless laughs in the form of wordplay, slapstick comedy, absurd situations and animal oddities that remind us of human behavior.

Kelly did not, however, initially identify the Okefenokee as Pogo's home. Numerous panels throughout the strip's run featured a tree of considerable size with a large root or two that grow aboveground and, in some cases, eventually dip into swamp water, reflecting the tangled roots that Vereen Bell mentions in his short story quoted previously. Early on, southern cities, including Nashville, Savannah, Atlanta and Tuscaloosa, appeared on the side of swamp boats in the comic strip, and the term *bayou* was used here and there, implying the strip was set in a Louisiana swamp. The precise setting didn't seem to matter as long as the reader understood that Pogo lived in a southern swamp. Eventually, though, the Okefenokee became the permanent home for the animals. A sign in a panel from *The Pogo Sunday Book* (1956) proclaimed, "The Okefenokee Glee-Pilau an' Fire Society Christmas Fry" in reference to a community meal put on by the local fire and chorus organization. In addition, Kelly described "the still waters of the Okefenokee Swamp, home of the Pogo people," in *The Pogo Papers*. One of the only place names of the Okefenokee rim used in the *Pogo* comic strip is Fort Mudge, a fort that was built during the Seminole Wars near the entrance to Cowhouse Island. While the fort was named for a soldier who was killed in a Native attack, Kelly undoubtedly borrowed "Mudge" for its humorous sound— the word combines *fudge* and *mud*—and perhaps because it also evokes the unstable, damp and dark-colored muck of the swamp.

Behind the swamp humor, however, lurked biting satire, as Kelly mocked hypocritical politicians and spoke out against the Vietnam War. Probably the most famous *Pogo* panel ran on Earth Day 1971; in it, Pogo pronounces the memorable line, "We Have Met the Enemy and He is Us," a revision of Oliver Hazard Perry's assertion during the War of 1812, "We have met the

The Waycross water tower with Pogo. *Larry Woodward, USFWS.*

enemy and they are ours." Pogo makes this claim to Porky Pine while they survey the garbage that humans have left behind in the swamp. After Kelly died in 1973, *Doonesbury* cartoonist Gary Trudeau wrote, "When Walt died, Okefenokee Swamp could never be the same."[110]

SILVER SCREEN AND SWAMP PARK

The fact that a generator was brought to the Hebard camp at Billys Island precisely so movies could be shown there indicates the central place that film had begun to acquire in the United States by the early 1920s. Although there are no records of what movies were shown on Billys, we can imagine that they included the typical fare for the time—the silent black and white films of Charlie Chaplin and Buster Keaton, for example, and perhaps even films that featured stories of strange goings-on in swampy wetlands, such as *The Secret of the Swamp* (1916), set in South America, and the Mary Pickford vehicle *Sparrows* (1926), which was set in an unnamed swamp and filmed in a Hollywood studio lot like the 1916 movie. As will be shown, the decision to film on location in a real swamp like the Okefenokee was sometimes made by directors who knew that no Hollywood set could rival the real thing.

The most significant example of how the beauty and mystery of the Okefenokee has lured film directors is the 1941 film *Swamp Water*, based on Bell's 1940 novel. Jean Renoir, son of the Impressionist painter Pierre-August Renoir, was the director. Renoir was already famous for his French films when he came to the United States to try out the Hollywood studio system. He quickly became discouraged with that system, which gave him much less freedom than he was used to in France. One thing that Renoir did insist on was doing some of the filming in the Okefenokee. Although studio executive Darryl F. Zanuck could not for the life of him understand Renoir's desire, he allowed the director and one of the actors, Dana Andrews, who played Ben Ragan, to spend time in Waycross and the swamp.

Swamp Water (1941), directed by Jean Renoir. This scene was filmed on a Hollywood set. *Left to right*: three unidentified men, Walter Huston, Eugene Pallette, Anne Baxter and Joe Sawyer. *Copyright 20th Century Fox/Photofest.*

Renoir loved meeting the swamp's locals and was impressed with them and their culture. In the swamp area, he felt he was finally experiencing authentic American culture. The opening scene of the film, especially, shows what Renoir could do with a film camera in the Okefenokee, as the camera shows a slow advance along the Suwannee Canal. A few more scenes of Ben were filmed in the swamp, but the rest was taped on studio lots, where Renoir also did the direction. He did not have input on other aspects of the film, however—not even on the crucial final editing. What we have with *Swamp Water* is, then, an uneven film with aspects of Renoir's and Bell's genius combined with Hollywood's clichéd depictions of rural life in a swampland.[111]

Like the book, the film introduces the Okefenokee as a place of danger, underscoring that no one has ever emerged from it alive. (In the book and film, no one actually lives full time in the swamp, as the Chessers did.) The swamp is truly menacing in the film, that menace represented by cottonmouths, gators and even quicksand. As for the storyline, the scriptwriter Dudley

Nichols's happy ending has Tom Keefer return with Ben to civilization, to his daughter and "to those that love him," as Ben says encouragingly. This happy ending stands in contrast to the end of the novel, in which Keefer, wounded, chooses to remain and die in the Okefenokee. As for the evil Dorsey twins, the true murderers, one dies in quicksand, and the other is abandoned; it is assumed he won't last long in the Okefenokee.

To convince Hollywood executives to host the premiere of the film in Waycross, the town sent them and others baby alligators, among other efforts. Their pleas were successful, and *Swamp Water* premiered on October 23, 1941, at both the Ritz and Lyric Theaters in Waycross. It was a huge affair and a perfect example of how local municipalities in the area have benefited from the lure of the nearby Okefenokee. Both Jean Renoir and actor Walter Huston attended. A Swamp Water Ball was held at the city auditorium, and a king and queen of the ball were selected at the Pilot Club. The Waycross Women's Club organized a celebration at the home of Jack Williams, the editor and owner of the *Waycross Journal-Herald*, and there was a Swamp Parade.

Just a decade after *Swamp Water*, another director was drawn to Bell's Okefenokee story. Jean Negulesco arrived in the United States from Romania in 1927 and directed *Lure of the Wilderness* in 1952. Thus, the two film versions of the novel were made by well-known directors from Europe. One difference between the versions is that Negulesco emphasized the Native aspect of the Okefenokee in ways that the book and the first film did not. Its opening credits are framed by clichéd markings that are meant to resemble Native symbols. This may have been an effort to draw on the popularity of Western films at the time. Already, *Swamp Water* had used the tune of "Red River Valley" as a gesture to Westerns. (Renoir had no input on the musical soundtrack.)

In *Lure of the Wilderness*, the female lead, Laurie, is not the Julie of Bell's novel. She is now center stage, or center swamp, living with her outlaw father in the Okefenokee instead of in town. She and her father, called Jim Harper instead of Tom Keefer (a role Walter Brennan played in both this film and Renoir's), have been in the swamp for ten years. Laurie does not know how "folks," meaning civilized people, live, Harper tells Ben. She is scantily dressed in animal skins and is ignorant of the ways of the world, making her the stereotypical Native "maiden" of many Western and adventure films. *Lure of the Wilderness* also premiered in Waycross but not without some finagling, according to local newspapers. It was originally scheduled to premiere in Atlanta, but Swamper Will Cox was evidently able to convince

Governor Talmadge to allow it to do so in Waycross, in part by visiting him with an Okefenokee snake. On July 16, 1952, the film opened in Waycross and the next day in Atlanta.

Swamp Water and *Lure of the Wilderness* are the most impressive in a series of Okefenokee films. The others, as will be discussed, were mostly B-movies, some tame, some sensationalistic, made on the cheap without the foundation of a serious literary achievement like Bell's novel and often without the assistance of Hollywood's studio personnel. Some of them are, nevertheless, entertaining, and their renderings of life in and around the Okefenokee are revealing.

Featurette is a term used to refer to medium-length (twenty-five- to fifty-minute-long) films produced for the most part before the late 1960s and shown on television or along with regular-length features in theaters. The featurette was meant to provide brief entertainment as a sort of preparation for a lengthier feature film. *The Living Swamp* (1955) is a thirty-three-minute 20th Century Fox featurette narrated by Dale Robertson and directed and cowritten by David DaLie. Filmed on location in the Okefenokee, it comes off as an advertisement for the Okefenokee Swamp Park (OSP). DaLie also stars in it, playing himself, as do Swampers Billy Dawson and Gideon Cox, both of whom were employed by the Swamp Park. Dale Robertson, who was known for appearing in television Westerns in the 1950s and 1960s, had also provided the voiceover narration at the beginning of *Lure of the Wilderness*. Another connection with Negulesco's film is that the actor who plays Ben, Jeffrey Hunter, was one of *The Living Swamp*'s producers. As will be seen, there were many connections between those who worked on Okefenokee movies and the OSP.

The Okefenokee, as a place to "get away from it all," to take a break from the ills of urban life, was marvelously captured in another featurette, a "travelogue" produced by the Ford Motor Company to promote the 1958 Edsel, one of the most memorable flops of the automobile industry. Entertaining and informative, *Okefenokee Interlude* presents the Okefenokee Swamp Park near Waycross as a stopover on a long car trip, in this case from somewhere north of Georgia to Miami. In just twenty-five minutes, viewers learn that the purchase of an Edsel, a sign of progress, can ironically provide them with a respite from progress by returning them to a place characterized by simplicity and harmony.

The story begins on the automobile assembly line, as the narrator confidently states, "This is the way some great adventures begin!"[112] When the car rolls off the line, it is quickly purchased by a northern doctor and his wife. The husband provides the rest of the narration, sharing his determination to escape his grueling job and annoying social obligations by heading toward Miami in the Edsel. Instead of showing the couple enjoying Miami, however, the movie focuses on their "off-the-track adventure." Traveling down U.S. Route 1, the main north–south artery on the East Coast in the 1950s, they stop at Waycross and then detour to the Okefenokee Swamp Park, just the "different world, primitive, mysterious, yet strangely satisfying" the doctor is seeking. On their boat ride through the swamp with a park guide (played by Swamper Will Cox), the doctor discovers the source of the Suwannee, expressing his feat as if he had found the source of the Nile: "Practically no one has seen it, even [Stephen C.] Foster, but *I'm* seeing it, right here and now!" Alligators, a bear, a snake and a gopher tortoise— the typical animals associated with the Okefenokee—greet the couple as the tour continues. After the tour, the couple and the guide travel in the Edsel to a Swamper cabin, where a family welcomes them to an outdoor meal. Neighbors soon arrive in a horse-drawn carriage, as opposed to the modern car. An old-fashioned "sing" delights the couple, who join in with the "nice folks" who are "plain, down to Earth," according to the doctor. After two hymns, "Amazing Grace" and "Old-Time Religion," the pair drive off. A copy of the Sacred Harp book that Will Cox has given to them sits between them on the car's front seat. Refreshed after this interlude, they are now relaxed enough to head to Miami. Most importantly, the doctor has discovered that "peace of mind can be found in simple things."

Folkston resident Sheila Carter has identified the man who first steps out of the wagon as her grandfather Harry Chesser, who is followed by other members of this famed Swamper family. Will Cox, as already noted, plays the boatman. After working for Hebard Cypress, Cox was a longtime guide at the Okefenokee Swamp Park. The travelogue thus incorporates living history into the film by having Swampers play themselves, though only Cox is credited. We can only wonder how many people were convinced to purchase the 1958 Edsel after seeing where it could take them!

In 1946, the Georgia legislature commemorated the life of native son Vereen Bell by naming the road that leads to the Okefenokee Swamp Park, east of Waycross, after him. The Vereen Bell Highway, also known as Okefenokee Swamp Park Road and Georgia 177, connects U.S. 1 to the park. A historical marker that tells the story of Bell's life is set up near the entrance sign. From the entrance, it is a seven-mile drive to the current visitors' center, where tourists can see wildlife and historical exhibits (including a recreation of Walt Kelly's study) and take guided boat rides into the swamp. OSP also runs Okefenokee Adventures, a boat tour and paddle adventure concessionaire, from the dock at the Suwannee Recreation Area of the Okefenokee National Wildlife Refuge.

OSP is a nonprofit organization that was founded in Waycross in the early 1940s. Local businesspeople, community leaders and Okefenokee enthusiasts shared an interest in promoting the area with a tourist and entertainment park, first on 1,200 acres of Cowhouse Island. In October 1946, the park was opened to the public. David DaLie, who was later involved in Okefenokee films, was appointed park manager and stayed in the position until 1954, when he left for California to pursue a career in entertainment. From its opening, the OSP was popular with locals and non-locals. In the month of July 1954, for example, 18,738 paying visitors explored it, despite what must have been high temperatures and humidity.

The swamp park in its early decades could be categorized as a "roadside attraction," one of many that sprang up around the United States during the automobile and local highway boom between the 1940s and early 1960s. Motorists stopped at these tourist sites on their way to vacation destinations, making the journey itself part of the fun. They picnicked, learned about local history and legends, watched their children let off steam and then got back on the road. Sometimes, these roadside attractions themselves were unusual structures; others drew families to see unusual natural sites, like the Okefenokee. As the interstate system of highways grew in the 1960s, especially, roadside attractions were bypassed, and they lost their appeal. Some have endured, however, and some have shifted their focus away from pure tourism. The Okefenokee Swamp Park belongs to this group, as it now works to promote educational outreach and wildlife research.

Jimmy Walker, whose great-grandfather was Obediah Barber, was manager at the Okefenokee Swamp Park starting in the mid-1950s, and he worked there until 1996. He was also a musician and leader of the band Jimmy Walker and the Swampers. Another familiar presence at the OSP was Richard "Dick" Flood, known as "Okefenokee Joe." Flood penned and sang environmentalist songs about the swamp and was also the park's animal handler. The shows he performed for families for many years were well attended, especially those that featured snakes and alligators, of course. Modifications to the OSP were made in the 1960s, including a new steel tower that replaced an older observation tower. In the 1970s, Pioneer Island and a new visitors' center were completed, and OSP also acquired more land. The swamp park's seventieth anniversary was celebrated in 2017 with Okefenokee Joe in concert. (It was postponed from 2016 due to Hurricane Matthew.)

"Nature's Wonderland," Okefenokee Swamp Park billboard, circa 1970. *OSP Archives.*

Many roadside attractions had mascots that were replicated in often oversized statues located—where else—on the side of the road. Live animals also became roadside mascots for use in exhibits and shows. The Okefenokee Swamp Park, like other animal parks in the past, kept a chained, docile animal—a bear—for guests to approach. Brown bears and alligators had long been identified as the most dangerous large creatures of the swamp, and the public was fascinated by them. In the 1950s, 1960s and even into the 1970s, a live bear mascot could be seen at OSP and could often be found "posing" with visitors for photographs.

One of the cruelest things done to the Okefenokee display bears—and this occurred not only at OSP—was that they were regularly encouraged to imbibe Coca-Cola, a beverage born in Georgia and manufactured throughout the state. Royal Crown (RC) Cola, another Georgia beverage, was bottled in Waycross and was sold at a stand at the OSP boat dock; it was also given to various bears. According to Luther Thrift (in a personal interview), twin bears Mitch and Teddy, sons of Swamper and Dynamite,

Rich's Department Store, Atlanta. Exhibit from the Okefenokee Swamp Park, circa the 1960s. *OSP Archives*.

drank a case a week of twelve-ounce RC Colas or Nehis. A popular postcard shows Mitch, who was chained by the boat dock, drinking from a bottle of soda. A female bear named June was also showcased. This practice stopped in the 1970s, when concern for the protection of the animals led to the end of such cruel practices in many places.

There have been two stuffed animal mascots at OSP, both male alligators. "Ole" Roy, who is mounted and on display, died in 1972 at about ninety years old after growing to be almost thirteen feet long and weighing 650 pounds. He was caught because he had a habit of craving the hauls of fishermen in the Suwannee Canal—and how could he not crave them? Roy lived his last twenty years in captivity at the park. He was named for Roy Moore, a manager of ONWR in the 1950s. Children and adults can now approach this once wild saurian mascot of the swamp in an exhibit room.

Oscar, a more recent resident of the swamp park, was not stuffed and mounted when he died; instead, his skeleton was preserved and meticulously reconstructed. Oscar never lived in captivity, but he was known to those

Cola bear, Okefenokee Swamp Park, circa 1960. *OSP Archives.*

who worked at the park for his regular appearances ever since the opening of OSP. When he died of natural causes in 2007, his skeletal remains were meticulously put together like pieces of a puzzle, and he was set and remains on display for visitors to ponder the internal architecture of the mighty alligator.[113]

This brief look at OSP's history prepares us to consider the films that have highlighted the Okefenokee, were filmed at the swamp park and/or involved OSP employees, as well as others that were also set somewhere in the swamp. They draw, like *Okefenokee Interlude*, on the "primitive" or lost-in-time aspect of the swampland. Swamplands are favorite settings (either real or constructed) for monster and creature movies, such as *The Creature of the Black Lagoon* (1954), *Swamp Thing* (1982) and their sequels (these were not set in the Okefenokee). Swamp terrains seem to naturally suggest myths and legends of outsized creatures, even half-human half-animal beings, who roam the soggy land. Okefenokee movies have been less about swamp creatures and more about escaped criminals, however. Both swamp creature and other

Roy, Okefenokee Swamp Park. *Larry Woodward, USFWS.*

Oscar, Okefenokee Swamp Park. *Larry Woodward, USFWS.*

B-movies about swamps are sometimes grouped as "swamploitation" films, meaning they are low-budget movies that rely on unusual and often lurid storylines and settings. Many could also be called adventure films.

The contrast between the two display alligators at OSP today—one stuffed, one a scientific display—demonstrates how the park's purpose has evolved to include major efforts in education. An educational film about the Okefenokee from 1986, *Realm of the Alligator*, was produced by National Geographic and narrated by Pernell Roberts, the star of the television series *Bonanza*, a civil rights activist and a native of Waycross. From the late 1940s to the early 1970s, though, the Okefenokee was a setting for mostly fictional films, some serious wilderness stories, some less serious B-movies. Like the Everglades, the Okefenokee has its share of silver screen versions. In the following paragraphs, we will become familiar with several kinds of movies that set their stories in the land of the trembling earth, some filmed near the OSP, and a few set elsewhere in the swamp.

In 1947, director Ewing Scott's *Untamed Fury*, a Danches Brothers production, was released. The film stars Gaylord (Steve) Pendleton as a Swamper who returns home with an engineering degree in hand and the goal of modernizing the Okefenokee by building canals. His antagonist is 'Gator-Bait Blair, thus nicknamed because his cruel father had used him (when he was a child) as alligator bait. Quicksand is part of the setting in this film, as it is in other swamp movies, although there is actually no quicksand in the Okefenokee. *Untamed Fury* features a stereotypical elderly Black man, "Uncle" Gabe, who sings "Nobody Knows the Trouble I've Seen." Also, notably, E.G. Marshall received screen credit for the first time as the "frolic" caller in this film. *Untamed Fury* had its premiere in Waycross at the Ritz theater.

Black Fury, a 1953 half-hour naturalist movie—not the feature film *Black Fury* from 1935—starred David DaLie. Directed by the Florida-based brothers Ted and Vincent Saizis, this movie is about the hunting and killing of a dangerous bear by a group of Swampers. The film poster introduced viewers to the Okefenokee as a savage place where man and wild animal do battle in "Nature's Most Dreaded Swampland."

Land of the Trembling Earth (1952), a featurette documentary directed by Ted Saizis and made in cooperation with the U.S. Fish and Wildlife Service, starred OSP employees Gideon Cox and Billy Dawson. When it premiered at Waycross's Lyric Theater in 1952, the swamp park bear Dynamite was photographed buying movie tickets. On the other hand, *Okefenokee* (1959), directed by Roul Haig, was a B-movie through and through. Its poster, which

Actor Dave DaLie at the Okefenokee Swamp Park with snake and advertisement for *Land of the Trembling Earth* (1952), a short film directed by Ted Saizis. Warner Brothers Production. *OSP Archives.*

mentions the Okefenokee, screams out, "Raw Passions in the Hell Swamps!" The story is about a Seminole Army pilot who returns to the swamp after a few years and discovers that a smuggling gang has taken control of the area—but not for much longer. The poster for *Swamp Country*, a 1966 film directed by Robert Patrick, boasts, "Actually Filmed in the Wilds of the Dreaded Okefenokee." The music in the film, including the songs "Swamp Country" and "Obadiah," was written and recorded by Jimmy Walker and his band. This movie also features criminal escapees in the Okefenokee, a motel called the Swamper, a bear and a title song sung by Baker Knight. It stars Lyle Waggoner and, not surprisingly, David DaLie. Rex Allen, a singing cowboy in B-Westerns, plays the sheriff.

Swamp Girl (1971) was directed by Donald A. Davis and is definitely a swamploitation film. When it premiered at the Lyric, Spanish moss was hung from the marquee, and a swamp boat was parked outside near the sidewalk ticket booth. Reportedly, the Obediah Barber home was used for filming. Country music singer Ferlin Husky stars as the park ranger, and the titular swamp girl, Janeen, is what we might call a lowbrow version of the Swamp Angel. Harrison Page plays her Black "Pa" who has run away from the law after being falsely accused of stealing a pair of pants. He tells Janeen that he saved her as a baby from an evil white slave trade doctor, whom he had worked for. When an escaped female convict arrives and shoots Pa, Janeen is forced to lead her out of the swamp. Fortunately, a handsome park ranger saves the day. This one has it all, including quicksand, a snake farm and an airboat.

David DaLie (1919–1995), a state deputy game warden and manager at OSP, was an actor in and writer of *The Living Swamp*, *Black Fury*, *Swamp Country* and *The Tender Warrior*. A wrestler, DaLie also performed stunts with alligators, bears and snakes at the swamp park. On a memorable day in June 1950, he dressed in swim trunks and wrestled an alligator on a trapeze over Okefenokee water. Called the "Tarzan of the Okefenokee Swamp," DaLie left the Okefenokee in 1954 to pursue an acting career, but he returned many times to be involved in swamp films. He also cowrote and starred in screen adventures set in South American jungles, where he handled crocodiles instead of alligators. He died in Palm Springs, California.

Swamp Girl and *The Tender Warrior*, both from 1971, are the last two of the series of Okefenokee adventure films from what we might call the heyday of Okefenokee Swamp movies. *The Tender Warrior*, a comedy and adventure film, brought together a typical group of Okefenokee locals: David DaLie cowrote the script; Charles Lee, the young star, grew up in Waycross; Jimmy Walker wrote and sang the title song; and Swampers Johnny Hickox and Liston Elkins (the latter worked many years at OSP) star. The non-locals involved included director and cowriter Stewart Raffill, originally an animal trainer, and who went on to make other wilderness adventure films. Rafill was involved in the *Tarzan* television series, and his animal background shows up in *The Tender Warrior* (the boy Sammy has a chimp as sidekick). Dan Haggerty, who gained fame later from *The Life and Times of Grizzly Adams* (1974), plays an animal trapper and moonshiner, the son of Liston Elkins's character. In *The Tender Warrior*, a boy discovers that illegal acts are being

The Tender Warrior (1971), directed by Stewart Raffill. *Safari Films/William Thompson Productions, Harry Ransom Center, University of Texas at Austin.*

committed in the Okefenokee by moonshiners and trappers, and he takes on the job of convincing the sheriff to intervene.[114]

Those interested in cultural productions associated with the Okefenokee rim will surely find it worthwhile to read Bell's novel *Swamp Water* and watch the two films made of it in 1941 and 1957. The novel contributes much to our current knowledge of life on the edge of the swamp in the past, and along with Bell's other writings, it offers a lyrical journey through this special wilderness. The films, especially Renoir's, demonstrate that nonlocals can make entertaining and well-shot stories and images of the land of the quivering earth. The less artistic films also offer an important glimpse into not only the way the swamp looked in the past but also how the makers of popular entertainment have conceived of the Okefenokee as a wetland ripe for consumption by popcorn-eating viewers. And although many of the characters portrayed in these movies are time-honored stereotypes, the presence of local Swampers and OSP employees gives us a very personal and valuable understanding of the way those closest to the Okefenokee have experienced it.

Opposite: *Left to right*: Larry Woodward (deputy project leader, ONWR), Emman Spain (NAGPRA coordinator, Muscogee Nation), Turner Hunt (historic preservation officer, Muscogee Nation), Richard Kanaski (regional archaeologist, USFWS), Susan Heisey (supervisory refuge ranger, ONWR) and Haley Messer (deputy regional archaeologist, USFWS). *Richard Kanaski, USFWS.*

CONCLUSION

In June 2022, members of the Muscogee Nation visited the Okefenokee National Wildlife Refuge and met with ONWR representatives. This was the first official visit of Nation members to the swamp since the days when the Muscogee were forcibly removed from the Okefenokee area. Turner Hunt, the tribal historic preservation officer and archaeologist, and Emman Spain, the NAGPRA coordinator for the Muscogee Nation's Historic and Cultural Preservation (NAGPRA is the Native American Graves and Repatriation Act of 1990), encouraged the preservation of this land, which is of great significance to the Nation. Leaders have been clear about their opposition to the proposed Twin Pines mining project on Trail Ridge, emphasizing the chance that it would disturb ancestral burial grounds, the same concern expressed by Interior Secretary Debra Haaland to Governor Brian Kemp in her letter.

It seems fitting to end this book with this extremely meaningful visit. Hopefully, we can ensure together that the Okefenokee Swamp, O-ke-fin-o-cau, remains a thriving ecosystem, one in which nature and humans can coexist in this most blissful spot on Earth.[115]

Water trail in the spring with cypress trees, Spanish moss, pond lilies and golden club. *Larry Woodward, USFWS.*

Suwannee Canal. In the fall, the needles of cypress trees turn orange and brown before dropping. *Larry Woodward, USFWS.*

Dawn on a water trail. These trails must be regularly cleared of aquatic plants. *Michael Lusk, USFWS.*

Supermoon on the Okefenokee. *Larry Woodward, USFWS.*

Longleaf habitat. This pine is the red-cockaded woodpecker's preferred tree for building a den. *Larry Woodward, USFWS.*

Billy's Lake. Boats from Stephen C. Foster State Park to Billys Island go across Billy's Lake. Pond lily flowers on this side of the swamp are mostly yellow. This plant is also called spatterdock. *Larry Woodward, USFWS.*

An aerial view of peat blowup and hammocks, or houses, in the swamp. Peat blowups create new trembling earth in the swamp. *Larry Woodward, USFWS.*

Swamp gas, also called bog or marsh gas, is caused by the decomposition of plant matter and peat formation below the surface of the water. It is actually methane gas. *Kenneth Murray and ScienceSource.*

Left: Patches of red on trees in the Okefenokee may resemble markers to indicate canoe trails, but they are actually examples of red Pyrenula lichen. *Courtesy of Walt Frazier*.

Below: Cypress knees grow vertically from the shallow, horizontal roots of the trees. There is no widely accepted function attributed to them. *Courtesy of Walt Frazier*.

American alligators can be seen along canoe trails. This reptile's skin is shiny and resembles armor. *Michael Lusk, USFWS.*

Alligators may be well hidden under the water's surface. Watch for their large eyes and bone bumps on their backs, called scutes. *Larry Woodward, USFWS.*

The gopher tortoise is a keystone species, meaning it has a central role in maintaining the ecosystem. *Larry Woodward, USFWS.*

A pig frog peers with its large eyes at a white pond lily flower. It is probably resting on a lily pad that is hidden underneath it. *Larry Woodward, USFWS.*

Left: An orb-weaving spider, also called a banana spider, may look dangerous, but it will most likely flee if you stumble into its web. *Courtesy of Peter Eimon.*

Below: The Okefenokee fishing spider is one of the largest spiders in the United States. It hunts for insects both on the surface of water and underneath it. *N. McMillan, USFWS.*

The golden club, also called neverwet, has tiny yellow flowers. It is seen with maidencane and ferns along boat trails. *Larry Woodward, USFWS.*

A pitcher plant. This carnivorous plant loves the Okefenokee habitat. Its colors are some of the most beautiful in the swamp. *Larry Woodward, USFWS.*

Above: The Okefenokee zale moth caterpillar has a restricted diet; without the fetterbush vine that grows on the buttresses of cypress trees, we would not see its magnificent colors. *Courtesy of Karen Chiasson.*

Left: The red-cockaded woodpecker is hopefully making a comeback in the Okefenokee uplands. *Larry Woodward, USFWS.*

In the uplands outside of the national refuge, red-cockaded woodpecker chicks are banded so that they may be monitored. The bands do not hurt their legs, even as they grow larger. *Kimberly Birrer, USFWS.*

Barred owls do not migrate. Lucky ones are born and live out their lives in the Okefenokee, where they can be seen in the daytime perched high on trees. *Larry Woodward, USFWS.*

Wood storks. This threatened bird is making a slow comeback in the United States. They are not solitary birds, so you will see them only in groups. *Larry Woodward, USFWS.*

This beautiful sandhill crane strikes a pose in front of saw palmettos. *Larry Woodward, USFWS.*

The Suwannee Sill at the headwaters of the river was constructed to raise the water level of the swamp. It is no longer used. Notice how black the Okefenokee's waters can look. *Michael Lusk, USFWS.*

An aerial view of the 2017 West Mims fire. National refuge employees used helicopters to drop water and to monitor fire. *Michael Lusk, USFWS.*

Above: The homestead on Chesser Island. Members of the Chesser family lived on this island for more than one hundred years. The fenced front yard was regularly cleared of leaves and brush to discourage snakes from approaching the house. *Larry Woodward, USFWS.*

Left: The chimney at Chesser homestead. *Courtesy of Walter Frazier.*

High Bluff Primitive Baptist Church is still active. *Larry Woodward, USFWS.*

Okefenokee Swamp Park entrance, vintage postcard, 1967. *M&N/Alamy stock photograph.*

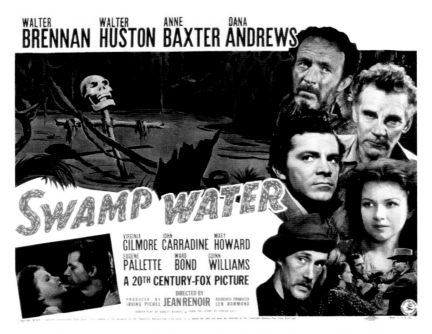

Swamp Water (1941), directed by Jean Renoir, with Walter Brennan, Walter Huston, Dana Andrews, Anne Baxter and John Carradine. *Copyright 20ᵗʰ Century Fox/Photofest.*

Lure of the Wilderness (1952), directed by Jean Negulesco, with Jean Peters, Jeffrey Hunter and Constance Smith. *Copyright 20ᵗʰ Century Fox/Photofest.*

NOTES

Chapter 1

1. Hawkins, *Creek Confederacy*, 21–22.
2. Wright, *Our Georgia Florida Frontier*, 6:1–7.
3. A 1967 note in the book by Francis Harper *Okefinokee Album* explains his preference. See Harper and Presley, *Okefinokee Album*, xv.
4. *Sixth Report of the United States Geographic Board*, 569.
5. "Statement of Universal Value." I thank Sara Aicher for providing me with this unpublished document.
6. On Trail Ridge, see Hoyt and Hails, "Pleistocene Shoreline Sediments," 1,541–43. A good source for information on the natural features, animals and plants of the Okefenokee is Schoettle's *A Naturalist's Guide to the Okefenokee Swamp*.

Chapter 2

7. Correspondence with Dr. Marcia Haag, professor of linguistics at Oklahoma State University, helped me understand these Choctaw terms, and I thank her.

Chapter 3

8. McQueen and Mizell, *History of the Okefenokee Swamp*, 142–43.

9. Harper and Presley, *Okefinokee Album*, 174–75.

10. Ibid., 175.

11. Trowell provides anecdotes about fires in the Okefenokee in his "Okefenokee's Great Wildfires."

Chapter 4

12. Bartram, *Travels*, 47.

13. Ibid., 48.

14. Ibid.

15. Wright, *Our Georgia Florida Frontier*, 6:3.

16. Ibid., 6:10.

17. For the history of Indigenous peoples in the Swamp, I rely largely on Trowell, *Indians in the Okefenokee*.

18. Cited in White, *Archaeology and History*, 113.

19. More information on this ceremony and other aspects of Creek life is available in Hawkins, *Creek Confederacy*, and White, *Archaeology and History*.

20. Bartram, *Travels*, 48.

21. Hawkins, *Creek Confederacy*, 9.

22. Ibid., 22.

23. Ibid., 14.

24. For the view of the term meaning "runaways" or "separatists," see Sprague, *Origin, Progress, and Conclusion*, 18–19.

25. Trowell, *Indians in the Okefenokee*.

26. Quoted in Trowell, "Exploring the Okefenokee: Letters from the Expeditions," 14–15.

27. On Floyd's march through the Okefenokee, see Trowell, "Exploring the Okefenokee: Letters and Diaries from the Indian Wars"; and Trowell, "General Charles R. Floyd and the Second Seminole War." In addition, Megan Kate Nelson devotes a chapter to the Second Seminole War and the Okefenokee in her book *Trembling Earth: A Cultural History of the Okefenokee Swamp* (40–70).

28. W.W.S. Bliss to the governor of Georgia, December 22, 1841. Letter reproduced in Sprague, *Origin, Progress, and Conclusion*, 413.

29. Governor McDonald to the secretary of war, March 10, 1842. Letter reproduced in Sprague, *Origin, Progress, and Conclusion*, 414.
30. Nelson, *Trembling Earth*, 73.

Chapter 5

31. On Ellicott's Mound, see Coulter, "Okefenokee Swamp: Part I."
32. Allen, "Allen's Journal," 1–57.
33. See Trowell, "Exploring the Okefenokee: The Richard L. Hunter Survey."
34. Coulter, "Okefenokee Swamp: Part II." Coulter gives a good overview of canal and drainage projects involving the Okefenokee.
35. Wilhoit, "Exploring Georgia's Wonderland."
36. Walker, "Biography of Dr. Frank Clingman Folks."
37. Trowell and Izlar, *Jackson's Folly*; Coulter, "Okefenokee Swamp: Part II."
38. Harper and Presley, *Okefinokee Album*, 189.
39. This section is partly informed by Trowell, *Hebard Lumber Company*; Trowell and Fussell, "Exploring the Okefenokee: Railroads of the Okefenokee Realm"; and Coulter, "Okefenokee Swamp: Part II."
40. Hopkins, *Forty-Five Years*, 1–69. Nelson's chapter on development in the Okefenokee, "El Dorado: Okefenokee and Dreams of Development," is also informative. See *Trembling Earth*, 71–115.
41. Wilhoit, "Exploring Georgia's Wonderland."
42. Harper and Presley, *Okefinokee Album*, 171.
43. Brundage, "Varn Mill Riot of 1891," 270.
44. Ibid., 262–63.
45. Ibid., 278.
46. Harper and Presley, *Okefinokee Album*, 189.

Chapter 6

47. Cited in Trowell, *Life on the Okefenokee*, 11–12 (brackets are Trowell's).
48. Francis Harper papers, Special Collections, Georgia Southern University, box 10, January 10, 1939.
49. McQueen and Mizell, *History of the Okefenokee Swamp*, 37.
50. Crowley, *Primitive Baptists*, 96–97.
51. Cited in Trowell, *Life on the Okefenokee*, 13.
52. Hopkins, *Forty-Five Years*, 25–26.

53. Ibid., 51.
54. Ibid., 51–52.
55. Caldwell and Bourke-White, *You Have Seen Their Faces*.
56. Harper and Presley, *Okefinokee Album*, 137.
57. Trowell's history of Billys Island is very detailed. See Trowell, *Billy's Island*.
58. Trowell, "Introduction to Okefenokee Place Names," 38–39.
59. Wright, *Our Georgia Florida Frontier*, 6:16.
60. It is also sometimes said "Tom Tiger" (Thlocklo Tustenugee) spent time in the swamp and even that the Seminole chief Osceola lived there for a time when he was young; this is not supported by the evidence. See Wright, *Our Georgia Florida Frontier*, 6:16–34, on Billy Bowlegs and Osceola.
61. Mays and Mays, *Queen of the Okefenokee*, 62.
62. Trowell, *Life on the Okefenokee*, 16.
63. Harper and Presley, *Okefinokee Album*, 74–75.
64. One of several sources for Obediah tales is Matschat, *Suwannee River*. More information on Swamper tall tales is available in part III of this book.

Chapter 7

65. McQueen and Mizell, *History of the Okefenokee Swamp*, 41.
66. Francis Harper papers in the Special Collections of Georgia Southern University, box 10, folder 37. A 1913 paper on the soils of the Okefenokee situates John's N-word Island as "lying northwest of scrub Island but not shown on map made last spring." See Carr, "Report Concerning the Soils."
67. Mays, *Settlers of the Okefenokee*, 39.
68. Hopkins, *Forty-Five Years*, 37.
69. Bohannon, "Guerilla Warfare."
70. Carlson, "Loanly Runagee," 607.
71. Pendleton, "Panther Fight," 5.
72. Harper and Presley, *Okefinokee Album*, 174 (brackets are Harper's).
73. Ibid.
74. Trowell summarizes much of this history in *Seeking a Sanctuary*.
75. Trowell, "Surveying the Route," unpublished notes, 1997.
76. Harper and Presley, *Okefinokee Album*, 8.
77. Trowell provides an overview of the Civilian Conservation Corps in the Okefenokee in his report that was published in *OWL News*, September 1999, 1–5.

78. Holland, interview with Henry Taylor. I'd like to thank Sara Aicher for sharing a copy of this transcript with me.

79. Jackson, "Haaland Voices Opposition."

Chapter 8

80. Harper and Presley, *Okefinokee Album*, 160–63.

81. Ibid., 138.

82. Cothran, "Talking Trash," 345–46.

83. Harper and Presley, *Okefinokee Album*, 94.

84. Pendleton, "Panther Fight," 2.

85. Ibid., 5.

86. Pendleton, *Atlanta Constitution*, October 31, 1875, 3.

87. Francis Harper's papers, Delma E. Presley Collection, Special Collections, Georgia Southern University, box 10, folder 2.

88. Harper and Presley, *Okefinokee Album*, 96.

89. Ibid., 97–98.

90. Thrift, *Tales of Ol'Ok-Fe-Nok*, 29.

91. Cothran, "Talking Trash," 350–51.

92. Crowley, *Primitive Baptists*, 180.

93. On Sacred Harp singing, in addition to Crowley, *Primitive Baptists*, see Sommers, "Hoboken Style."

94. Crowley, *Primitive Baptists*, 99, 179.

95. Harper and Presley, *Okefinokee Album*, 130.

96. The quotes are found in Francis Harper's papers, Delma E. Presley Collection, Special Collections, Georgia Southern University, box 10.

97. Harper and Presley, *Okefinokee Album*, 62.

98. Thrift, *Tales of Ol'Ok-Fe-Nok*, 45.

99. Harper and Presley, *Okefinokee Album*, 60–61.

100. Ibid., 56.

101. Ibid., 37.

Chapter 9

102. David C. Miller provides a much more detailed account of the various meanings swamplands acquired for Americans, at least in the nineteenth century, in his book *Dark Eden* (1989). I was fortunate to meet with him and discuss swamps in 2014.

103. "Charles Pendleton probably visited the island in 1893 with his brother Louis, but they left no account unless the description in Louis Pendleton's articles and book *In the Okefinokee* was based on personal observation during their rainy trip to Billys Island and surrounding swamp during mid-February 1893. Much of the information was based on Charles Pendleton's 1875 articles. The writers noted that Indians were trapping on Floyds Island at the time of their trip to the swamp." Trowell, *Floyds Island Hammock*, 20. The spelling in the novel's title is actually "Okefenokee."

104. Pendleton, *King Tom and the Runaways*.

105. Pendleton, *In the Okefinokee*.

106. Bell, "Way the Swamp Looks," 211–12.

107. Bell, *Swamp Water*.

108. Ibid., 6.

109. McQueen, *Club-Foot of the Okefenokee*.

110. See Kelly's collections *The Pogo Papers* and *The Pogo Sunday Book*, as well as Garry Trudeau's introduction to Mrs. Walt Kelly and Bill Crouch Jr.'s *The Best of Pogo*.

Chapter 10

111. Sesonske, "Jean Renoir in Georgia," 24–66. Sesonske's article is a thorough look at the film and Renoir's time in Waycross and the Okefenokee.

112. I thank Sheila Carter for mentioning this film to me during a conversation on the porch of the Chesser homestead. She and her daughter, Charlene, who was also present, are descendants of the Chessers.

113. Oscar can be seen enjoying the waters of the Okefenokee in the 1977 short, "Legendary Okefenokee Swamp Man." The legendary swamp man is Okefenokee Swamp Park guide and superintendent Johnny Hickox.

114. Johnny Hickox also appeared in a 1964 episode of *Mutual of Omaha's Wild Kingdom* called "Land of the Quaking Earth." The episode also features Joe Morton, the Okefenokee National Wildlife Refuge manager at the time, and James V. Hall, an ONWR aide. Like other Okefenokee films, this was a group effort of both insiders and outsiders.

115. See Ray Glier's article in the *Georgia Recorder* and the U.S. Fish and Wildlife Service article.

SELECTED BIBLIOGRAPHY

Allen, Alexander A. "Allen's Journal: A Trip Along the Georgia-Florida Boundary, June 14–July 22, 1854." Edited by Christy T. Trowell and Frances R. Trowell. *Occasional Paper from South Georgia* no. 6 (1984): 1–57.

Bartram, William. *Travels of William Bartram*. New York: Dover, 1955.

Bell, Vereen. *Swamp Water*. Athens: University of Georgia Press, 1981.

———. "The Way the Swamp Looks." In *Brag Dog and Other Stories*. New York: Armed Services Edition Inc., 1943.

Bohannon, Keith. "Guerrilla Warfare during the Civil War." *New Georgia Encyclopedia*. August 14, 2020. https://www.georgiaencyclopedia.org/articles/history-archaeology/guerrilla-warfare-during-the-civil-war/.

Brundage, W. Fitzhugh. "The Varn Mill Riot of 1891: Lynchings, Attempted Lynchings, and Justice in Ware County, Georgia." *Georgia Historical Quarterly* 78, no. 2 (Summer 1994): 257–80. https://www.jstor.org/stable/40583032.

Caldwell, Erskine, and Margaret Bourke-White. *You Have Seen Their Faces*. New York: Arno Press, 1975.

Carlson, David. "The 'Loanly Runagee': Draft Evaders in Confederate South Georgia." *Georgia Historical Quarterly* 84, no. 4 (Winter 2000): 589–615. https://www.jstor.org/stable/40584305.

Carr, M. Earl. "A Report Concerning the Soils of a Portion of the Okefenokee Swamp." 1913. https://ecos.fws.gov/ServCat/DownloadFile/27084.

Cothran, Kay L. "Talking Trash in the Okefenokee Swamp Rim, Georgia." *Journal of American Folklore* 87, no. 364 (October–December 1974): 340–56. https://www.jstor.org/stable/538970.

Coulter, E. Merton. "The Okefenokee Swamp: Its History and Legends. Part I." *Georgia Historical Quarterly* 48, no. 2 (June 1964): 166–92. https://www.jstor.org/stable/40578461.

———. "The Okefenokee Swamp: Its History and Legends. Part II." *Georgia Historical Quarterly* 48, no. 3 (September 1964): 291–312. https://www.jstor.org/stable/40578402.

Crowley, John G. *Primitive Baptists of the Wiregrass South: 1815 to the Present.* Gainesville: University Press of Florida, 2013.

DaLie, David, dir. *The Living Swamp.* 20th Century Fox, 1955.

Davis, Donald A., dir. *Swamp Girl.* Donald A. Davis Productions, 1971.

Glier, Ray. "Will Confirmation of Suspected Tribal Burial Grounds End Okefenokee Mine for Good?" *Georgia Recorder*, June 15, 2022. https://georgiarecorder.com/2022/06/15/will-confirmation-of-suspected-tribal-burial-grounds-end-okefenokee-mine-for-good/.

Haig, Roul, dir. *Okefenokee.* Filmservice Distributing Corp., 1959.

Harper, Francis. "Okefinokee Swamp as a Reservation." *Natural History* 20, no. 1 (1920): 28–41.

Harper, Francis, and Delma E. Presley. *Okefinokee Album.* Athens: University of Georgia Press, 1981.

Hawkins, Benjamin. *Creek Confederacy and a Sketch of the Creek Country.* Orlando, FL: Alpha Editions, 2021.

Holland, Dennis. Interview with Henry Taylor. October 18, 1998.

Hopkins, John M. *Forty-Five Years with the Okefenokee Swamp: 1900–1945.* Atlanta: Georgia Society of Naturalists, 1946.

Hoyt, John H., and John R. Hails. "Pleistocene Shoreline Sediments in Coastal Georgia: Deposition and Modification." *Science* 155, no. 3,769 (March 1967): 1,541–43. https://www.science.org/doi/10.1126/science.155.3769.1541.

Jackson, Gordon. "Haaland Voices Opposition to Mining Near Okefenokee." *Brunswick News*, December 9, 2022. https://thebrunswicknews.com/news/local_news/haaland-voices-opposition-to-mining-near-okefenokee/article_c72bc569-5b8d-5532-81ee-4ddee8894caf.html.

Kelly, Walt. *The Pogo Papers.* New York: Simon and Schuster, 1953.

———. *The Pogo Sunday Book.* New York: Simon and Schuster, 1956.

Lanier, Virginia. *Death in Bloodhound Red.* Sarasota, FL: Pineapple, 2007.

Matschat, Cecile Hulse. *Ladd of the Big Swamp: A Story of the Okefenokee Settlement.* Philadelphia, PA: John G. Winston, 1954.

———. *Suwannee River: Strange Green Land.* New York: Literary Guild of America, 1938.

Mays, Lois Barefoot. *Settlers of the Okefenokee*. Folkston, GA: Okefenokee Press, 1975.

Mays, Lois Barefoot, and Richard H. Mays. *Queen of the Okefenokee*. Folkston, GA: Okefenokee Press, 2003.

McQueen, A.S. *Club-Foot of the Okefenokee*. Atlanta, GA: Pegasus, 1939.

McQueen, A.S., and Hamp Mizell. *History of the Okefenokee Swamp*. Clinton, SC: Jacobs and Co., 1926.

Miller, David C. *Dark Eden. The Swamp in Nineteenth-Century American Culture*. Cambridge, UK: Cambridge UP, 1989.

Mutual of Omaha's Wild Kingdom. Season 3, episode 1, "Land of the Quaking Earth." Aired October 18, 1964. NBC.

National Geographic. "Realm of the Alligator." 1986.

National Park Service. "National Register of Historic Places Inventory–Nomination: John M. Hopkins Cabin." 1983. https://npgallery.nps.gov/GetAsset/59c82eda-abab-42f4-9355-24d0ef8e1264.

———. "National Register of Historic Places Registration Form: Floyds Island Hammock-Hebard Cabin." 2000. https://npgallery.nps.gov/GetAsset/2ec9bca0-257c-4810-9756-16a562a28007.

Negulesco, Jean, dir. *Lure of the Wilderness*. Los Angeles: 20th Century Fox. 1952.

Nelson, Megan Kate. *Trembling Earth: A Cultural History of the Okefenokee Swamp*. Athens: University of Georgia Press, 2009.

Okefenokee Interlude. Travelogue film. Allen Park, MI: Edsel Division, Ford Motor Company, 1958.

The Original Georgia Traveler. "Legendary Okefenokee Swamp Man…Johnny Hickox." Andy Johnston, narrator. WSB-TV Atlanta. 1977. https://www.youtube.com/watch?v=VLLDGfT8rlE.

Patrick, Robert, dir. *Swamp Country*. Patrick-Sandy Productions, 1966.

Pendleton, C.R. *Atlanta Constitution*, October 31, 1875, 3.

———. *Atlanta Constitution*, November 12, 1875, 2.

———. "A Panther Fight. Uncle Ben in the Jungles of the Okeefenokee." *Atlanta Constitution*, September 18, 1888, 3.

Pendleton, Louis Beauregard. *In the Okefenokee. A Story of War Time and the Great Georgia Swamp*. London: Forgotten Books, 2012.

———. *King Tom and the Runaways: The Story of What Befell Two Boys in a Georgia Swamp*. New York: D. Appleton, 1890.

Raffill, Stewart, dir. *The Tender Warrior*. William Thompson Productions/Safari Films, 1971.

Renoir, Jean, dir. *Swamp Water*. Los Angeles: 20th Century Fox, 1941.

Saizis, Ted, dir. *Land of the Trembling Earth*. Burbank, CA: Warner Brothers, 1952.

Saizis, Ted, and Vincent Saizis, dirs. *Black Fury*. Burbank, CA: Warner Brothers, 1953.

Schoettle, Taylor. *A Naturalist's Guide to the Okefenokee Swamp*. Darien, GA: Darien Printing and Graphics, 2022.

Scott, Ewing, dir. *Untamed Fury*. Cleveland, OH: Danches Brothers Production, 1947.

Sesonske, Alexander. "Jean Renoir in Georgia: *Swamp Water*." *Georgia Review* 36, no. 1 (Spring 1982): 24–66. https://www.jstor.org/stable/41398391.

Sixth Report of the United States Geographic Board: 1890–1932. Washington, D.C.: United States Government Printing Office, 1933.

Sommers, Laurie Kay. "Hoboken Style: Meaning and Change in Okefenokee Sacred Harp Singing." *Southern Spaces*. August 17, 2010. https://southernspaces.org/2010/hoboken-style-meaning-and-change-okefenokee-sacred-harp-singing/.

Sprague, J.T. *The Origin, Progress, and Conclusion of the Florida War*. London: Forgotten Books, 2015.

"Statement of Universal Value." Proposal to make the Okefenokee Wildlife Refuge a World Heritage Site. July 2022.

Thrift, J. Luther. *Tales of Ol' Ok-Fe-Nok. Legendary Stories of the Okefenokee Swamp*. Waycross, GA: Brantley Printing, 1999.

Trowell, C.T. *Billy's Island: A Historical Sketch*. Folkston, GA: Okefenokee Wildlife League Special Publication no. 2, 2000.

———. "Civilian Conservation Corps Company 1433 and the Development of the Okefenokee National Wildlife Refuge." *OWL News*, September 1999.

———. "Exploring the Okefenokee: Letters and Diaries from the Indian Wars, 1836–1842." *Occasional Paper from South Georgia*, no. 5 (1992).

———. "Exploring the Okefenokee: Letters from the Expeditions in 1875." *Occasional Paper from South Georgia*, no. 4 (1989).

———. "Exploring the Okefenokee: The Richard L. Hunter Survey of the Okefenokee Swamp 1856–57." *Occasional Paper from South Georgia* no. 1 (1988). Revised 2003.

———. *Floyds Island Hammock: A National Register of Historic Places Site*. Folkston, GA: Okefenokee Wildlife League no. 8, 2018.

———. "General Charles R. Floyd and the Second Seminole War in the Okefenokee Swamp." 1996. https://web.archive.org/web/20150610195622/http://www.glynngen.com/~thecrypt/history/floydseminolewar.html.

————. *The Hebard Lumber Company*. Folkston, GA: Okefenokee Wildlife League Special Publication no. 5, 1998.

————. *Indians in the Okefenokee: Their History and Prehistory*. Folkston, GA: Okefenokee Wildlife League Special Publication no. 2, 1998.

————. "Introduction to Okefenokee Place Names." Unpublished report. 2013.

————. *Life on the Okefenokee Frontier*. Waycross, GA: Okefenokee Wildlife League Special Publication, no. 3, 1998.

————. "Okefenokee's Great Wildfires." Unpublished report. 2007.

————. *Seeking a Sanctuary: A Chronicle of Efforts to Preserve the Okefenokee*. Folkston, GA: Okefenokee Wildlife League Special Publication no. 6, 1998.

————. "Surveying the Route of the Proposed Okefenokee Scenic Highway." 1935. Unpublished notes, 1997.

Trowell, C.T., and Lorraine Fussell. "Exploring the Okefenokee: Railroads of the Okefenokee Realm." *Occasional Paper from South Georgia*, no. 8 (1998).

Trowell, C.T., and R.L. Izlar. *Jackson's Folly: The Suwanee Canal Company in the Okefenokee Swamp*. Folkston, GA: Okefenokee Wildlife League Special Publication no. 4, 1998.

Trudeau, Garry. "Introduction." In *The Best of Pogo*. Edited by Mrs. Walt Kelly and Bill Crouch Jr. New York: Simon and Schuster, 1982.

U.S. Fish and Wildlife Service. "Muscogee Nation Visits 'Most Blissful Spot of the Earth.'" July 14, 2022. https://www.fws.gov/story/2022-07/muscogee-nation-visits-most-blissful-spot-earth.

Walker, Laura Singleton. "Biography of Dr. Frank Clingman Folks." Laura Singleton Walker Collection, Okefenokee Regional Library System.

White, Max E. *The Archaeology and History of the Native Georgia Tribes*. Gainesville: University Press of Florida, 2002.

Wilhoit, Lloyd A. "Exploring Georgia's Wonderland." *Atlanta Constitution*, November 27, 1921.

Wright, Albert Hazen. *Our Georgia Florida Frontier*. Vol. 6. *The Okefenokee Swamp, Its History and Cartography*. Parts 1–6. Ithaca, NY: A.H. Wright, 1945.

ABOUT THE AUTHOR

Marie Lathers grew up in Silver Spring, Maryland, and spent summer vacations with her grandmother in Waycross, Georgia. Her first question when she arrived there was always, "When are we going to the Okefenokee?" Unlike her friends at home, she was never afraid of alligators—up to a point. Lathers holds advanced degrees in literature and has spent thirty-five years teaching literature, film and French to university students, mostly at Case Western Reserve University in Cleveland, Ohio. She has written scholarly books and articles and is trying her hand at creative writing for children. She lives in New Smyrna Beach, Florida, and is happy to be relatively close to the Okefenokee Swamp.

Visit us at
www.historypress.com